Dr. Lloyd T. Commins

## An Expert's Smart Strategy Guide to:

# WINNING AT CRAP$

*Melvin Powers*
*Wilshire Book Company*

12015 Sherman Road, No. Hollywood, CA 91605

REVISED EDITION

1965

---

Manufactured in the United States of America

ISBN 0-87980-345-2

This book is dedicated to my good friend Dave Paulson, who through his many visits to Reno, Nevada, and his extreme lack of knowledge of percentages on Dice, has inspired the writer to write this book on Bank Crap;

To my good friend John Galvin, who has spent many a dollar purchasing books on Crap in which the authors exhibit little or no knowledge or practical experience of the game, and specialize in mis-statements and phony systems;

To my many friends who enjoy going to Reno and Las Vegas to shoot Crap.

# HOW TO SHOOT CRAP TO WIN

This book is a manual for Crap shooters, whether professional or amateur.

It deals with casino gambling in Crap, giving you percentages and methods of play including all propositions: Six and Eight, Field, Line Betting, Don't Pass, Come and Don't Come, as well as various combinations.

You will learn the value of odds and the distinction between Place Betting and Come Betting. No one should risk a dollar on a Crap Table without full knowledge of the contents of this book.

# Foreword

The writer of this book would feel amiss, if he failed to advise on an efficient procedure for digesting its contents to the fullest extent.

The average layman would not attempt to read a book on law or chemistry hurriedly and justifiably feel as though he had full knowledge of the subject at hand. If such be the case, why then should he attempt to do that with this book, which is based on mathematics?

It is for this reason that I would recommend your reading the book through carefully at least once. Then make a study of its contents. Start with the first lesson and, after acquiring complete, detailed knowledge, proceed to the next step, using —wherever possible—a pair of dice for practical purposes.

One must realize, in writing a book of this type, that three distinct classes of people must be taken into consideration:

The individual who is unfamiliar with the game of Crap and requires a fundamental education on the subject, thus necessitating considerable detail.

The individual who thinks he knows the game and always loses because he has no knowledge of percentages, and is of the opinion that it is all based on luck.

The seasoned or experienced player, who over a period of time has developed a sense of procedure, which has been acquired from expensive, repeated playing. This player has some idea of percentages, but does not know exactly what they are or how to decipher them. His answer to technical questions regarding percentages is, "It's a bad bet." It is because of his ignorance of percentages that he himself makes many bad bets.

From the above, you can readily realize that a detailed knowledge of percentages is absolutely essential; it is needless to mention the word "luck," if there is such a thing. Some prefer to call it cycles, which have a tendency to follow an extreme, regardless of percentage or common sense. It is these cycles, which go from one extreme to another, that must be recognized and taken advantage of, in conjunction with percentage. This makes a successful crap shooter. Take heed, do not invest your hard-earned money without a thorough knowledge of what you are doing, and then only if conditions are to your liking.

All investments require thorough knowledge and a good sense of perspective.

Dr. Lloyd T. Commins

# Contents

# HOW TO SHOOT CRAP TO WIN

## Introduction

## Bank Crap

Literally, a *bank* is an institution dealing in money, such as loans or exchange.

Crap is a game played with two dice, usually for money. Bank Crap, as universally understood, means a gambling game operated by a casino, which banks or finances the game against the players.

This author does not like the word "gambling." To him, gambling means to take a chance. Gambling casinos take no chance; they take a percentage of every play. In this world of ours, finance is one of the world's greatest institutions, and in every community we have some edifice which is situated on the most valuable piece of land, and which stands out because of its massive, elaborate construction. This is known as a "bank." All its wealth and success are derived from a small rate of interest. This interest or percentage is the backbone of the financial world, which is represented by our banks.

So is it that percentage is the backbone of the multi-million dollar casinos that operate the Bank Crap game.

Every bet permitted in a Bank game is a percentage, no matter how small, in favor of the Bank. Sometimes so trivial, we ignore them, sometimes so great that they flabbergast one. On top of all this, quite like taxes, there are many hidden percentages.

It is upon those two small unimportant dice that empires are built. Yet Solomon, in all his wisdom, could not predict each and every roll of these two small, inert cubes. But many people do know and realize the average reaction or percentage, over a period of time.

It is upon these reactions and percentages that this author is attempting to show you how the game is played, and the percentages taken from the player by the Casino through the various percentages.

These Bank games are legal and operated under the strictest supervision, unlike the private games, known as a Fading Game, among a group of individuals.

In mentioning the Fading game, which we do *not* intend to discuss in this book, it would be amiss not to mention the name of Harry Conamar, a one-armed dice man who could make dice perform like trained seals.

This author was born in San Francisco in 1899 and has lived in that vicinity up to the present time.

San Francisco was noted in those early days, as the *only city* west of Chicago, and the gambling center of the world, with its Barbary Coast and its waterfront, its North Beach and its Mission District, where Crap games were as common as cigar stores are today.

Every district had Crap games (Fading game) almost every day, usually starting out with 5 and 10¢ bets, not to mention the Big Games that were held every night throughout the city for the High Rollers. Most all of these games were played with honest dice, and practically everyone knew the other fellows. Every stranger was watched in every move he made, even unto blowing his nose. Everyone knew odds and percentages and gambled in the hope of being lucky. It is true, that the professional, because he had the bankroll, got the better of the play and his share of the flat bets, as he was in a position to lay a sizeable bet on the odds.

On the other hand, there were groups who specialized in crooked dice and set traps for the suckers. Some of the notorious places were the Sunday picnics that surrounded the Bay Area, and there was a picnic every Sunday, to be sure. Of these, the most notorious was Glen Park in San Francisco. As kids, we would climb over the fence to gain entrance to the picnic grounds and spend our time down

14

by the creek, watching the professional hustlers ply their trade of crooked dice. To us, this was fascinating, as we knew who had the crooked dice and could time just the moment they were to enter the game. The cleverness of manipulation was astonishing. Then again, there was the group who had the concession on the waterfront, ready at a moment's notice to clip the newly arrived seaman, or the drunk, or whatever worthwhile prospect that arrived on the scene.

Each kid had a trained eye for crooked dice, and if he picked them up and got a close look at them, he seldom missed.

There were other ways of accomplishing the purpose of winning, one of which was with a Shot, which means, one who could throw the dice (Fair Dice) and, by spinning or manipulating them in devious ways, throw any number he so desired with almost every roll of the dice. All of the shots and details of crooked dice are very ably explained in detail by John Scarne in his book on dice.

It was from the Fading Crap game, which was supposedly originated by John Crappaud among the colored people in New Orleans, that the present Bank Crap game developed. John Winn of New York, a gambler, is the accepted originator of the Bank Crap game in about the year 1907. He ran a game, similar to the Fading game, but the House took all the over bets and charged a five percent Vigorish Charge, as he called it. That is, if you wanted to bet $10 on your shot and had no takers, the Bank would take your bet, but would charge you 50¢ for taking the $10 bet. He also originated permission for the Wrong Bettor to bet that the dice would not pass, bar two 6's, plus the five percent Vigorish Charge.

It was through Mr. John Winn that the importance of perfect dice became such a vital factor in a Bank Crap game, as the player could either bet the dice Right (Do Pass) or Wrong (Don't Pass). However, it is needless to mention that Mr. Winn had a percentage in his favor, whether the

15

players bet the dice Right or Wrong, plus the additional five percent he got for accepting the bets.

All of these steps and perfections are the foundation of the present Bank Crap game, as it is played today, besides the many propositions that are presented to the suckers, which vary into fantastic percentages in favor of the Bank or House, as you might call it.

Let us go back to our author.

It was from watching these games of Crap, and whenever the opportunity presented itself, play himself, that the author got to know the percentages of dice, just as he knew his A B C's. Yet, without being present, if you told him there was a Crap game in a certain location, he would ask, "Who are playing?" and could tell you if the game was crooked or not, and who were handling the phony dice, that is, in the vicinity of the well-known San Francisco haunts.

Contrary to authors, who tell you fantastic stories about crooked dice and crooked games, and of gamblers being taken for wads of money, this is not true, as a gambler knows the game, its percentages, its dice, and never plays in such games. Most gamblers are honest and not cheats.

Yet with all the knowledge of gambling that the Big Players had, particularly Crap, each night at 12 P.M. they would gather at Willie Conroy's Cigar Store to play among themselves. Willie Conroy's Cigar Store closed at 11:30 P.M. every night. The front door was locked and all the front lights put out, but the back room was loaded with people discussing fights or playing cards.

Once the front door was locked, all those arriving would enter through a narrow passageway between the two buildings. It had a small door locked from the inside, ably guarded by Old Sport, a character who knew everyone by his first name, as well as his life's history.

At the appointed time, Mike, a surly former police sergeant, walked out with his hat on, and assumed his position in back of a large table, which was the signal for the game to start.

In those days, some of the most frequent visitors were, Joe Gleason, Whitey The Barber, Jew Morris, George Gazock, known also as the Turk; the Pelsinger brothers, Harry, Dave and Sam, all former prize fighters; Mike Catalano, Tex Frank O'Brien and George Wienholtz, and at one time the well known Nick The Greek.

This of course was a Fading Crap game. Each fellow shot the dice and paid 50¢ on Two Passes, or if he passed the dice, he threw Mike a half-dollar. This was about the biggest crap game in San Francisco. The players would Fade the Center and lay or take the odds. Such bets as $500 to $1000 he makes his Point No. 4 were very common. Many of the players had from $20,000 to $30,000 cash in their pockets, each one hoping to get lucky and make a cleanup. Willie Conroy's was the Clearing House for the Crap shooters. Outsiders could and did play, but never was there such a thing as crooked dice.

When Nevada legalized gambling, Reno was the largest gambling center in the New World. Most of Reno's business came from San Francisco and the Bay Area—all smart players.

The laws regarding cheating are very strict in Nevada; they not only have individuals watching who are players, but also state men who are specially trained in every phase of crookedness. You can rest assured that, under the circumstances, no million-dollar concern is going to risk loss of its license for just a few paltry dollars. Yes, it has been tried in several out-of-the-way places, and then mostly with cards. These places no longer exist.

A Gambling Casino is a business house and, if you are treated with respect and consideration, and the surroundings appeal to you, that is the place you transact your business.

The game that is herein described is a Bank Crap game

as is conducted in Reno, Nevada. Other places have slight variations, but if you understand the Game of Crap as the author intends that you do, any slight variations in other places are immediately recognized.

It is the author's intent that you not only read this book, but study it so that you are thoroughly familiar with every detail and can answer any question that might arise pertaining to the Game of Crap. Once you have attained this objective, you will not lose large sums of money and will have an excellent chance of winning, but never Break the Bank, as they have millions in reserve.

Always remember that the element of luck, plus percentage, excels. If two men were guessing the flip of a coin, one selecting heads and other tails for a given period of time, there would be no percentage, but the element of luck would be on the winner's side. If this were continued for a long period of time, each man would have won an equal number of times, because luck would be eliminated, and percentage, which is equal, would prevail.

It is with this thought in mind that I will proceed, giving all the information you need to play the Game of Crap as it is played in Reno, Nevada.

*Good luck to you.*

# Chapter 1

## History of Bank Crap Game

At the request of many close friends who frequent Reno and Las Vegas, Nevada, for the purpose of gambling, I am writing this article on the most popular game—Crap.

This article in no way is written for the purpose of encouraging gambling, but on the contrary, to enlighten people as to what they are doing and how to minimize the percentage against them, so that it is possible for them to win. It is needless to mention that many people who play this game cannot win, because of their lack of knowledge of the game.

The story of dice goes back to before the time of Christ and is most prominently mentioned by the Saviour of mankind dying on the Cross on Calvary, when He said, "And they cast lots for my garments." Today, the country of Monaco is supported by the gambling casino of Monte Carlo. Prince Rainier and his wife Princess Grace live in fabulous wealth in the country of Monaco, supported by gambling, while his subjects are tax free. Compare this to the taxes paid by the average citizen of any city or hamlet in the greatest country, America, with the exception of but one state, Nevada, where gambling is legalized.

At the discovery of the Western world, gambling was introduced. On the West Coast, from San Francisco to Alaska, gambling was one of the most prominent enterprises, and it played an important part in the development of the West. It was to this that many of our prominent citizens owe their fortune and success. Yet today it is illegal, and has been for a good many years, with the exception of the state of Nevada.

Through all these years, people have made a study of how to beat the game of dice, but have failed because of one word—Percentage.

Some have tried loaded dice, which were soon detected; others have used tops and bottoms, which are dice that are switched into the game and have only numbers that will not make a Seven. Others have tried shading dice, or trimming off one or the other side to unbalance them, thus favoring certain numbers. All of these have failed, and today a crook, with all of his devious devices, is absolutely helpless in a gambling casino.

To give you some idea of a pair of dice in a gambling casino: each die is squared with calipers to a degree of perfection, so that each side is absolutely flat, and any two sides are the same thickness. This is vitally important, as the professionals, either player or casino owner, base their success on percentage.

Today, you have a great many women dealers. This has only a psychological effect on the players, as most people think of a professional gambler as a man who is very deft in the handling of dice and cards, as we see in the movies. Truthfully, a dealer has nothing to do with the dice, except collect or pay off as the numbers come up. Of course, each die has a secret mark on it to prevent some unscrupulous person from attempting to switch in a pair of crooked dice. You will note, if one of the dice rolls off the table, the dealer immediately looks for the mark, before giving it to the player to continue. In most gambling casinos, the dice are changed every eight hours, with different marks, which are only known to the dealers of that table. The reason for the constant changing of the dice is that they may become nicked hitting money on the table, and therefore would be off, which might favor certain numbers and be detrimental to either the player or the house, depending on the nicks.

I wish to emphasize again that dice are absolutely on the square, and the house works on the basis of percentage. This word percentage is one that will appear throughout this book and in every play.

If the reader expects the writer to give him a foolproof system so that he cannot lose, he can stop right here, because if that were possible, all of these multi-million-dollar casinos would close tomorrow, and the writer would become wealthy, and not waste his time trying to give you his secret. Yet you can read article after article that will give you systems that are infallible, and all of them are untrue.

This writer is trying to tell you the truth, that is, that the game is based on percentages and to show you *why,* and that if you play with the minimum of percentage against you, and are consistent, you have a good chance to win— but only a limited amount, and not break the bank.

Before going into the detail of the playing of this game, perhaps it is best that we make a quick survey of the gambling casinos and their clientele.

In Las Vegas, you have the Strip, which is made up of casinos on both sides of the highway from the Hotel Flamingo, Sands, Desert Inn and Thunderbird, some of the new ones that cost millions of dollars. In town, you have the old established Golden Nugget.

The cost of construction, as well as operation, is far beyond the scope of the average visitor. Each of these plush casinos serves excellent food at a very low cost, as well as the world's greatest entertainment, all within the range of the average pocketbook. The entertainment by the outstanding stars is superb, because money is no objective; and the salaries paid these entertainers are higher than any place in the world.

New York, with its huge population, which at one time controlled all the world's best entertainment, is second only to Las Vegas. These facts about entertainment are mentioned only to show you that the player is the important factor. Another factor that enters into the cost of operation and advertising is the excursion offered by the different casinos, which is about half to one-third the normal cost.

Many of these excursions give you money or chips on arrival to get you started. The above factors are termed advertisements.

Yet, the actual cost of operation of a casino is tremendous. To mention some, the state tax on a crap table is $100 per day. State and government tax on profits, plus employment and free drinks given away hourly in many casinos, as well as free entertainment, all enter into the cost of operation. With all the above advertisements as overhead, we then come down to the crap table, which is where all the "big money is bet."

Each table is operated on a 24-hour basis. Usually two dealers, sometimes a croupier (stick man) with a dealer on each side, who pay off bets or rake them in as the dice are rolled. Some casinos have a pit man or overseer, who walks around in back of every crap table, or sometimes the pit man sits on a high chair, looking like a referee at a tennis match. Other places have sloped glass windows high on the wall, which look like mirrors. These are not the mirrors they appear to be, but windows where they can see out and watch every player, as well as the dealers. All of this is to prevent stealing or mistakes, or any funny business that might exist or be anticipated by either the dealers or the players. If one added the cost of operating one crap table in a casino, it would be amazing. The cost would vary from casino to casino, but to give you an idea, it would run from $700 to $1000 per day, which is a conservative estimate, not counting the advertisements used to bring the players to the casino. Plus all these mentioned articles, there are shills.

# Chapter 2

## Shills

A shill is a person who is given money by the house or casino just to play. Psychologically, an individual does not want to go up to a table and play by himself, because he feels as though he is a sucker, and everyone has the trap all set for him. Yet if there are several people playing, he is encouraged, feeling as though he has company. These shills are usually women, very attractive, and in many cases divorcees, who are killing time during their six-week waiting time. Each shill is paid a salary of about $5 per hour. They work two hours on, 15 minutes off, for eight hours. They are given $20 by the house and can only play $1 at a time, and on the Line only. As they place their $20 on the rack provided for players on the rim of the table, you will note that they stack $5 upright, $5 flat, $5 up and $5 flat, so that at a glance the dealers can note just how much money the shill has. No one, shill or dealers, is allowed to put his hand in his pocket. If they desire to blow their noses, the house has Kleenex available. Also, you will note that before even attempting to pick up the Kleenex or take their hands off the table out of sight, they must show the palms of each hand first, then rub them together and turn them over. The reasons are obvious.

## Chapter 3

## The Man Who Made a Living
## Shaking Dice Out of a Box

Another thing that might intrigue you with the Crap Table is the handling of the dice. Years ago, most gambling casinos had a dice box, which they passed from shooter to shooter as the game progressed. This has long been discarded, because, through years of practice, some professionals have been able to throw any number they desired out of the dice box into the middle of the table, not only out of a dice box but out of their hand. This was only done when the dice did not hit the sides of the table. However, with the dice box, it appeared to the average amateur that control of the dice was lost, when thrown out of the box. This was not true.

I once knew a man who traveled throughout the country, making a good living shaking dice in cigar stores. It was done in just the same way we frequently see today in bars, fellows shaking for a drink. This fellow would go to a cigar store, requesting a package of cigarettes, place his money on the counter, and then suddenly say to the owner, "I'll shake you double or nothing." This was good business for the storekeeper, and he usually consented. They would take a dice box, as you so often see, and start to shake. Needless to mention, this man could control all five dice in the box. I have actually seen him throw five 6's on request in one roll. As to the storekeeper, it seemed as though it was just a bad day for him, being beaten by the smallest margin. Sometimes this expert would leave with an armful of cartons of cigarettes. Other times, after losing so much, the keeper would get suspicious and excuse himself to go in back

24

for a moment. He would then phone the police, come back and continue with the game, awaiting the arrival of the police.

To show you how sharp a professional is, our man had a confederate working with him. Long before the police had time to arrive, he would signal his confederate across the street through some simple gesture, like tipping his hat. The confederate would rush in, flash a phony star and ask the storekeeper if he had phoned the police. The keeper would be delighted to think that he was instrumental and so smart as to catch a crook. The confederate, a phony police officer, would gather up all the merchandise, put handcuffs on the professional dice man, and haul him off to jail—or so the storekeeper thought. On the contrary, the two would go on to the next town, and work the same gag over again as they crossed the country. This is a true story.

Now you see why gambling casinos do not use a dice box but make the shooter throw the dice full length of the table, so that the dice will hit the far railing or wall of the table. In so doing, one loses all control of the dice.

You will note that no matter how crude a shooter is, man or woman, the dealer will stop the dice, if they do not hit the back wall, as they say. This hitting of the back wall, with complete loss of control, puts the throw of the dice back on a percentage basis, upon which this game of Crap is based.

You will also note that all the racks of the dealers contain only silver dollars and chips. Recently because of silver shortage, chips of $1 valuation have replaced the silver dollars. These chips are of but four denominations—$5, $20, $25 and $100. The dealer never has any paper money. All money bets are paid off either in silver or chips, according to the bet. All paper money bet or given to the dealer for change is placed in a slot in front of the dealer and disappears into a locked container underneath the table. At the conclusion of a play, wherein the player decides to cash in, he must leave the table and go to the cashier's window to exchange either silver or chips for paper money.

These chips and silver, used in playing, have a very significant value, to the casino's advantage, which is an increased percentage. This statement may seem ridiculous, but a fact.

For example, if a player were paid off in greenbacks, he would in many instances put them in his pocket, and thus unconsciously end up a winner. Silver is too heavy to put in his pocket; therefore, he leaves it on the table. As for the chips, they soon lose all value, and the player continues to play until he is wiped out. Can you imagine a woman walking up to a table and putting $1 on Eleven at 15 to 1, and the dealer giving her a $10 and a $5 greenback? Nine out of every ten would put the money in their pockets and walk away. On the contrary, the dealer pays her $15 in silver dollars and leaves her $1 on the Eleven for the next roll. The result is, she continues to play, with a great percentage against her. As you know, percentage is not based on only one roll of the dice; but over a period of time it proves itself.

Therefore, with a big percentage against a player, the house must end up with the money.

I hope that I have briefly given you a picture of the operations of a casino, its cost of construction, its methods of operation and its personnel, which in many cases consists of as high as 1000 employees in one casino, and I hope to show you the necessity of the gambling casinos' demand for a volume of "sucker play" over a period of time.

The writing of a book of this type is most difficult, depending on the reader or student. If one is a novice, it requires many simple details, which are known to the experienced crap player and gambler and may appear to be monotonous to them. But a review of the details herewith may also be helpful in bringing to light trivial details that may be taken for granted or overlooked, yet very important. Therefore, our first bit of advice in shooting crap is *study the game,* and know every percentage and angle of it before you play.

## Chapter 4

## Cardinal Rules of the Crap Player

I think it would be well at this point to set up rules or cardinal principles that are absolutely essential for a successful crap shooter. In so doing, I am going to shock many an experienced player and gambler, as they themselves are frequent violators of the cardinal principles set forth. Yet the majority of them agree that they are vitally important.

Cardinal Rules:

1. Never get into a game without $200 cash on hand to invest.
2. Never buy less than $100 in chips at a time.
3. Never lose more than you can afford.
4. Never drink before or during a play.
5. Decide how much you can afford to lose before you start to play, and stay with it.
6. Never hesitate to quit a game, if you are loser and things are running bad.
7. Never hesitate to quit a game, if you are winner and the dice turn against you.
8. Never bet less than $5.
9. Always take double odds on every bet.
10. Never vary your pattern of play.
11. Aim to quit with a profit.

12. Never go to your pocket or purse for additional money, once your $200 is lost.

It might be well, at this point, to dispel all thoughts as to crookedness in a gambling casino. One should just stop and think that a gambling house with a million-dollars-a-month income would not take a chance of losing its license to win $500 on any crooked venture, knowing the Gaming Commission is watching at all times.

# Chapter 5

## Dealers and Their Methods of Handling Bets

All dealers go to school to learn the operation of a crap game. They are taught not only the game, but how to handle the public, particularly under stress. The majority of dealers, both men and women, are good looking, are well dressed, and have a pleasing disposition. Believe it or not, most dealers like to see you win. Why? Because they feel sorry for the average sucker. Secondly, if a man plays the game as it should be played, it is exactly the pattern that they themselves play when they get in a game, and therefore they feel that this type of player should win. I have actually seen, in a big casino in Reno, four big bettors playing, and the dealer called the floor manager to request a change of dice, because the dice were missing continually. All four bettors awaited the arrival of the new dice, before they continued the game.

It is common among both patrons and dealers to get to know each other very intimately, as well as every play that the player is going to make in his pattern of play. If, through distraction, the player overlooks a play, the dealer will call his attention to it. The result is that a good player, on winning, will compensate the dealer on leaving. I have seen a player throw as high as $150 to the dealers on quitting a game after a good win. So you see, the dealer is there to do a job, and by being courteous and nice to the players, he sometimes receives several times his salary for his day's work, plus the fact that the management receives nothing but compliments for having such capable, well-mannered dealers.

Always remember, it is human to make mistakes, therefore watch your bets and the amount of your payoff. Some dealers are thieves at heart and cannot help but short-change a sucker, or the management of an unscrupulous casino may send in a dealer to take the drunken sucker by shortchanging him. These cases are rare, but do occur.

Another point that might be interesting to you is, How Do the Dealers Keep Track of the Bets? Who's Who? To start with, each dealer is only dealing to half the table; therefore, the bet belongs to a player on his half. Second, each player, unknown to himself, follows a pattern of play, soon recognized by the dealer.

For example, there is a Field player or a Wrong bettor, a Come bettor, Six and Eight, or the one who jumps around, but the important factor is the amount. If you have three or four players betting similar amounts on the Come, he faces the money toward the player who has made the bet.

For example, on a Come bet, suppose there are four bets of similar amounts on the same number, some with odds, and others without odds, all made by different players, on his half of the table. What he does is place the bet on the right-hand corner of the square pointing at the player to his right. He does the same to the player on his left, and to those directly in front of him, puts the bet in the center opposite the player. Whichever player takes odds, he places odds half balanced on the original bet.

Illustration:

A, B, C, D are the Players

Naturally, each Player should watch his own bets. Whenever there is a question as to whether it is your bet or not, ask the dealer prior to the roll of the dice.

# Chapter 6

## Claim Agents

A claim agent is one who claims other people's bets, hoping that by argument he will get the money, or that the House, for peace sake, will pay him off. These people are soon recognized by the dealer and the players. If this happens too frequently, the dealer refuses his bets or presses the buzzer for the floor manager, who escorts him out.

The average dealer, in an eight-hour shift, will change $100,000 from paper money into either chips or silver. The amount of money he handles, in paying off bets and collects, runs into an unbelievable amount, depending on the size of the game.

Watch your bets, count your money, know what you are doing and be pleasant.

So much for the operation of a Casino.

# Chapter 7

## The Game Itself

If an inexperienced player would take two dice and set them on a table before him, he would find that each die contained six numbers from 1 to 6, and that a pair of dice, as they are rolled out, will stop with one number on each die. Therefore, on two dice there are six times six combinations, which may come up or 36 different combinations.

So, if two dice are placed side by side, one rotating while the other remains stationary, we would have following combinations. For example, all the possible combinations with one die facing up and remaining stationary while the other is rotated:

1 on stationary die and 1 on the other equals....2

1 on stationary die and 2 on the other equals....3

1 on stationary die and 3 on the other equals....4

1 on stationary die and 4 on the other equals....5

1 on stationary die and 5 on the other equals....6

1 on stationary die and 6 on the other equals....7

2 on stationary and 1 on the other equals.......3

2 on stationary and 2 on the other equlas........4

2 on stationary and 3 on the other equals.......5

2 on stationary and 4 on the other equals.......6

2 on stationary and 5 on the other equals.......7

2 on stationary and 6 on the other equals........8

3 on stationary and 1 on the other equals.......4

3 on stationary and 2 on the other equals........5

3 on stationary and 3 on the other equals.......6

3 on stationary and 4 on the other equals........7

3 on stationary and 5 on the other equals........8

3 on stationary and 6 on the other equals........9

4 on stationary and 1 on the other equals........5

4 on stationary and 2 on the other equals........6

4 on stationary and 3 on the other equals........7

4 on stationary and 4 on the other equals........8

4 on stationary and 5 on the other equals........9

4 on stationary and 6 on the other equals......10

5 on stationary and 1 on the other equals........6

5 on stationary and 2 on the other equals........7

5 on stationary and 3 on the other equals........8

5 on stationary and 4 on the other equals........9

5 on stationary and 5 on the other equals......10

5 on stationary and 6 on the other equals......11

6 on stationary and 1 on the other equals........7

6 on stationary and 2 on the other equals........8

6 on stationary and 3 on the other equals........9

6 on stationary and 4 on the other equals......10

6 on stationary and 5 on the other equals......11

6 on stationary and 6 on the other equals......12

Thus is shown the possible numbers and combinations that can come up in throwing out a pair of dice—36 combinations—taking note that the number 7 is the only number that can come up with any number on the opposite die.

# Chapter 8

## Chart on Combinations and Odds

Thorough knowledge of this chart is absolutely essential to have any idea of percentages in the game of Crap. Yet, the Odds are the basic factor of the game. Therefore, learn them thoroughly before ever attempting to play the game. There are two types of Odds.

The more commonly referred to Odds are the possible chances of throwing the Shooter's Point before he throws 7.

The other types of Odds are the possibilities of throwing, IN ONE ROLL, any designated number. This is commonly referred to as Propositions.

As you know, there are 36 different combinations, that is, six sides on each die, which is 6 × 6 = 36 possible combinations in one roll.

The reason for this chart is to show you the true Odds on the various combinations, frequently referred to as Propositions, set forth on the gambling table. These Odds are based on the number of ways that the combination should be made to equal the number in one roll.

Propositions are an added sucker attraction that pays a high percentage to the House and yet seemingly offers fantastic returns to the Player for a small investment. MOST PROPOSITIONS ARE ONE ROLL BETS, and can be made on every roll of the dice, thus continued action regardless of who is shooting the dice or what his Point may be.

For example, there is one way of making the number 2 in one roll with a pair of dice; that is, one on one die and one on the other. As there are 36 combinations, you subtract the one way possible to make the number 2, which leaves 35 ways that it cannot be made with the dice.

Therefore, the correct Odds are 35 to 1. Yet take a combination such as 7, where it can be made six ways. The Odds would be calculated by subtracting the six ways from the 36 possible combinations, which would leave 30 possible combinations that it could not come up; therefore, you divide the 6 into 30, which gives you 5. And the correct Odds are 5 to 1 that you do not throw a 7 in one roll.

However, what is generally referred to as Odds, once a player or shooter gets a point, which is 4, 5, 6, 8, 9, 10, are the Odds against his making that point before he throws Number 7.

Odds are based that the Shooter throws a 7 before his Point. There are three ways of throwing a 4 and 6 ways of throwing a 7. Therefore, the Odds are 6 to 3 or 2 to 1 that the Shooter throws a 7 before he throws a 4.

| Shooter's Points | Odds |
|---|---|
| 4 | 2 to 1 |
| 5 | 3 to 2 |
| 6 | 6 to 5 |
| 7 | |
| 8 | 6 to 5 |
| 9 | 3 to 2 |
| 10 | 2 to 1 |

These numbers are all Points, which are the Shooter's Point or Line after the first roll. Once a Shooter has a Point, he either makes it and wins on the Line—or throws a 7 and loses. Therefore, all Odds are based that the Shooter will throw a 7, for the reason that 7 can be made more ways than any other number—six ways. The closest to it are 6 and 8, which have five possible combinations, thus the Odds 6 to 5 that you make a 7 before either 6 or 8.

Now that we see all the combinations that are available and have made an actual survey of the dice themselves, we have noted that some combinations can come up more frequently than others. It is the frequency of these combinations that is the basis of Odds. Unfortunately, everyone just wants a system to win or beat the game. But as I showed you in the beginning, the game is not there to beat and, furthermore, you must make an intricate study of the game to know what you are doing and why, otherwise your money is a gift without a chance to win.

Without going further, I know many people will disagree with this statement, explaining that they themselves or friends have won, yet they know nothing of the game. That I will agree on, because in the parlance of gambling there is an adage, Luck overcomes all percentages. Therefore, some suckers win at anything, regardless of odds against them. However, at the conclusion of this thesis, I will give you two systems; one in betting the dice Right (will pass), and the other betting the dice Wrong (do not pass); but you must understand all percentages that I am attempting to show you, before you can bet either way correctly and win. I will also give you a combination play, where you bet both Right and Wrong on the same number, and either break even or win on this play.

From the picture of a Crap Table on the following pages, you see nothing but numbers, with wording designating what you are betting on, all of which is very confusing to the newcomer. Therefore, I am going to take and dissect the Crap Table, giving you a complete understanding of what each group of figures or numbers mean, and the Odds.

# CHART ON COMBINATIONS & ODDS

| Numbers Possible | Combination that Makes the Number | | | | | Number of Ways to Make the Number | Odds on One Roll |
|---|---|---|---|---|---|---|---|
| 2 | 1&1 | | | | | 1 | 35 to 1 |
| 3 | 2&1 | 1&2 | | | | 2 | 17 to 1 |
| 4 | 1&3 | 3&1 | 2&2 | | | 3 | 11 to 1 |
| 5 | 1&4 | 4&1 | 2&3 | 3&2 | | 4 | 8 to 1 |
| 6 | 1&5 | 5&1 | 2&4 | 4&2 | 3&3 | 5 | 6-1/5 to 1 |
| 7 | 1&6 | 6&1 | 2&5 | 5&2 | 3&4 | 6 | 5 to 1 |
| 8 | 2&6 | 6&2 | 3&5 | 5&3 | 4&4 | 5 | 6-1/5 to 1 |
| 9 | 3&6 | 6&3 | 4&5 | 5&4 | | 4 | 8 to 1 |
| 10 | 4&6 | 6&4 | 5&5 | | | 3 | 11 to 1 |
| 11 | 5&6 | 6&5 | | | | 2 | 17 to 1 |
| 12 | 6&6 | | | | | 1 | 35 to 1 |

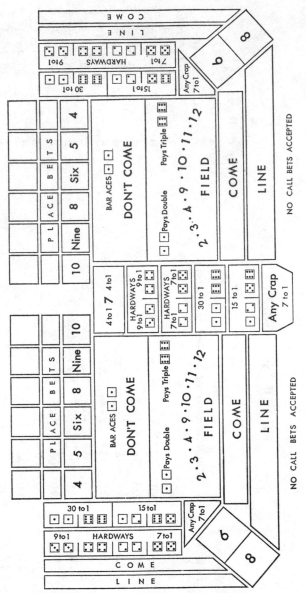

Picture of an Entire Crap Table

38

When a Shooter throws a Point, either 4, 5, 6, 8, 9 or 10, the Dealer places a large ring, acting as a marker, on that number indicating the Shooter's Point.

These large numbers in front of the dealer are also used to place Come bets and Place bets made by various players.

The blank squares in back of each number are used to place Don't Come bets, signifying the number the player is betting against.

# Chapter 9

## Propositions

The reason for having two halves in a Crap Table is that people on either half can play without trying to make a bet on the opposite end. The center portion of the table, as well as each end, also contains Propositions such as: Two Aces or Two Sixes, quoted at 30 to 1. Eleven or Ace Deuce at 15 to 1, Any Crap at 7 to 1 and the Number 7 at 4 to 1.

The reason for this type of layout is to encourage sucker bets by not only a visual reminder but by convenience.

You will also find "Hardways" among this group of Propositions. These are NOT one roll Propositions. Hardway quotations are odds paid by the House on even numbers or pairs required to make a specific number regardless whether it is the Shooter's Point or not.

For example:

|            |        | *Odds*  |
| ---------- | ------ | ------- |
| Two Deuces | (2 2)  | 7 to 1  |
| Two Treys  | (3 3)  | 9 to 1  |
| Two Fours  | (4 4)  | 9 to 1  |
| Two Fives  | (5 5)  | 7 to 1  |

At any time during the game, a player can place a bet on any or all of these numbers, regardless of the Come-Out or Point the Shooter may have. These are foolish bets, with odds against the Bettor. To explain why—go back to the chart on numbers and odds. For example, you bet on Two Treys, which is the Number 6. There are six ways or combinations to make a 7 and only five combinations to make

40

a 6, yet of the five combinations to make a 6 you pick one, which is Two Treys. Now, in the course of throwing the dice, if a 7 is thrown, you lose; if a 6 is thrown in one of the combinations—4&2 or 2&4 or 1&5 or 5&1—you lose again. No other numbers count or have bearing on this bet. So without being a great mathematician, you can lose on any 7, which can be made six different ways, and lose on making 6 four ways of the five possible ways to make it. Therefore, you can lose your money any one of ten combinations and win one way (Two Trey), so the odds should be 10 to 1. But in making the bet, you are taking 9 to 1. Thus percentage is very lopsided against the Player and in favor of the house. It is a very, very bad bet.

# Chapter 10

## Field

The next section to be analyzed is in the center of each half of the table. It is marked off and placed in a very prominent position, covering the largest part of the table; it reads "FIELD." The Field is a one-roll bet. In other words, you win or lose on each roll of the dice. The Field numbers are 2, 3, 4, 9, 10, 11, and 12.

This appears very attractive, with so many numbers in your favor; also, the fact the notation that Two Aces pays *double* and Two Sixes pays *double*. Let's go back to our chart:

### Winning Field Numbers

| Number | Ways of Making It |
|--------|-------------------|
| 2 (Aces) | one |
| 3 | two |
| 4 | three |
| 9 | four |
| 10 | three |
| 11 | two |
| 12 | one |

You can readily see that you have sixteen ways of winning. Again, we go back to our chart:

## Losing Field Numbers

| Number | Ways of Making It |
|:------:|:-----------------:|
| 5 | four |
| 6 | five |
| 7 | six |
| 8 | five |

Our chart shows we can lose twenty ways and win but sixteen, notwithstanding that we get paid double on aces and sixes. So this bet again proves that it is a very bad bet for a Player to make and is strictly a sucker bet, played only by a novice. Some casinos pay triple on two sixes.

Can you imagine the percentage and profit on each roll of the dice at the rate of 300 throws per hour? Yes, reader, the thought that flashed through your mind of doubling up won't work and will be discussed later.

# Chapter 11

## Crap—Seven-Eleven

Again, looking back at our picture of the Crap Table, we see on each half of the Table, and in the center, divided into small squares, such quotations of Odds as:

| Two Aces | 30 to 1 |
|----------|---------|
| Two Sixes | 30 to 1 |
| Any Crap | 7 to 1 |
| Eleven | 15 to 1 |
| Seven | 4 to 1 |

These are all one roll plays and can be bet on at any time, or on every roll of the dice. So again, we must go back to our master chart to check the Odds.

Of the 36 combinations that can be thrown, only one combination will make *Two Aces,* therefore, the correct Odds are 35 to 1. So you are taking 5 points the worst of the bet, or 16-⅔ per cent in favor of the House. Two 6's or 12 are identical in Odds, combinations and percentages, as are Two Aces.

*Any Crap* means a combination of Two Aces, Two 6's and Ace Deuce (1&2), or 2&1 (Deuce & Ace).

Our Chart shows the following:

Two Aces is but one of 36 combinations, therefore 35 to 1;

Two 6's is but one of 36 combinations, therefore 35 to 1;

Ace Deuce & Deuce Ace are two of 36 combinations, therefore 17 to 1.

So, from simple deductions, you can readily see that the only combination you can win on Any Crap is—

Two Aces one combination ........................................ 1
Two 6's one combination ............................................ 1
Ace Deuce & Deuce Ace, which is two combinations.... 2

Total number of combinations to win on Any Crap.... 4
Total number of combinations on dice .................... 36

Therefore, 4 divided into 32 leaves 8, and the Odds are 8 to 1 on this bet. Yet the House will lay you but 7 to 1. This is again another one of those truly sucker bets.

*Eleven*—The House lays 15 to 1.

There are two combinations to make Eleven, 6&5 and 5&6, which is 2 divided into 34, or 17. Thus the correct Odds, 17 to 1, are 11¼ per cent in favor of the House. Another bad bet.

There is considerable difference between 15 *to* 1 and 15 *for* 1.

Most small places pay 15 *for* 1, which means $14 plus the $1 bet gives you a total payoff of $15.

15 *to* 1 means the House is laying 15 against your $1, which is a total payoff of $15 plus $1, or $16.

The same applies to all Proposition Bets, which increases the percentage in favor of the House.

Some places pay 15 for 1 which is a decrease of $1 on every bet. Therefore, the Player unknowingly loses $1, because he does not know the difference between the wording of *to* and *for*. All reputable casinos pay 15 *to* 1.

To the average amateur or newcomer, all of these Odds appear fantastic and are therefore attractive; but you never see an experienced Player place a bet on any of these types of Plays, because the percentage is much against him. To give you an idea of how fantastic the Odds are, the House will lay you 15 to 1 the Eleven will not come up, and will lay you 240 to 1 that it does not come twice in succession. This quotation is not marked on the Table, but it is simply manipulated by the Player. For example, if you place $1 on Eleven, it pays 15 to 1. By the simple proceduce of leaving the $16 on Eleven, when it comes up for the second time in succession you get back 16 times 15, or $240, plus $16 bet. So you see, by this simple manipulation, you can get back $256 for $1. On all other combinations of this type, you can get fantastic Odds that the combination does not

45

occur twice in succession. Even on such a number as 7.

To break down the occurrence of 7 twice in succession, it works like this: place a bet on 7, which pays 4 to 1, permitting the $5 to remain; if the 7 is thrown again, you get 4 times $5 or $20, plus $5 bet. This shows you the Odds that the House will lay against any number occurring twice in succession, including the most common of all—number 7.

# Chapter 12

## Six and Eight

On each corner of each half of the Crap Table are two large squares which read "Six" in one square and "Eight" in the other. These are even-money bets. These bets one can make at any time, placing a bet or removing it, as the Player sees fit. When you make this bet, which pays even money, you are betting that the Shooter of the dice will make the number you bet on before he throws a 7. Bear in mind that each 6 or 8 are separate bets. For example, if you bet $2 on number 8, it makes no difference what the Shooter's Point is, or if he is throwing the dice out for the first time, or Come Out, as it is called. If the Shooter throws 8 you win and if he throws 7 you lose. The same applies to the Number 6. This bet is *not* a one-roll affair, and nothing that the shooter throws has any effect on this bet, other than either 8 or 7. He can throw ten Craps, but it does not affect your bet. Again, let's go back to the chart.

There are six ways of making 7, and only five ways of making 8; therefore, the Odds are 6 to 5 he does *not* make it. The same applies to the 6. Now you see you are taking even money on a 6 to 5 bet, which is another big percentage in favor of the House, a bad bet for the Player. Again, the thought comes about doubling up. Again, I ask you to wait, and we will go into that later.

47

# Chapter 13

## Main Part of Crap Game

Now to explain the main part of a Crap Game.

A player can either bet the dice "Right" or "Wrong." That is, he can either bet that the Shooter of the dice wins, whether it be himself or a fellow Player shooting the dice, or wrong, that the shooter loses, whether it be himself or another Player shooting the dice.

The line is a striped area about a foot from the wall of the Table and about three inches in width, running around three sides of the table (except the side of the table where the Dealers stand). The back of the money racks do not have the Line, because no player is eligible to stand in that section. A Shooter is not eligible to shoot the dice until he makes a bet either on the Line or behind the Line. (Don't pass.)

When betting on the Line, he is betting that the Shooter wins, whether it be himself or another Shooter. The minimum bet is usually $1, and the maximum is usually $400, though this varies. They have some 10¢ crap games. Also, the limit may be increased on request for "high rollers" or Big Money Bettors.

# Chapter 14

## Points

To start the progress of a Play, the Bettor, for example, bets $1 on the Line. He throws the dice on the signal from the Dealer and the game is on. If on the first roll he throws two aces, ace-deuce, deuce-ace, or two sixes, he loses. If he throws 7 or 11, he wins. In the case of a loss on the Line, the Dealer scoops all the money on the Line. In the case of a winner, the Dealer pays off the Line, being very careful to place an equal amount of money alongside the original bet.

If the Player throws any other number than the winning or losing numbers above, it becomes his Point. He continues to throw the dice until he has either made his Point (number) or throws a 7. If he makes his Point, he continues with the dice until he loses, that is, he fails to make his Point. Every time he wins, betting starts over, the Dealer paying off the Line even money, an amount equal to that which is bet. However, if a Player makes a Pass (winner), and then on his next throw (Come Out) he throws a Crap (two aces, ace-deuce, deuce-ace or two sixes) he holds the dice, if he so desires, or he may pass them.

The next Shooter is not compelled to shoot the dice, but may bet anyway he desires. To simplify the game, the Shooter, and all those playing the Line, win on 7 or 11 on the first roll, or lose on 1 and 1, 1 and 2, or 6 and 6. Any other number that comes up is his Point. He can roll any number of times, with but one way to win—make his Point, or lose only one way by throwing a 7.

As explained in the previous paragraph, you lose on Crap,

which is two aces, deuce ace, ace deuce or two sixes, which is four ways to lose on the Come Out.

On the win side of the Come Out, you have 7, which has six ways, and 11, which has two ways. Therefore, there are eight ways to win on the first roll and four ways to lose (Crap) on the Come Out. So if you have eight ways to win on the Come Out and four ways to lose on the Come Out, the first roll is vital, because 8 and 4 are 12, which is one-third of the 36 combinations. The result is that you have 24 possible combinations for a Point on the Come Out. Therefore, it is a 2 to 1 bet that the Shooter throws a Point rather than a natural (7 or 11) or a Crap (2, 3 or 12) on his Come Out—his first roll.

# Chapter 15

## Wrong Betting

This section or square on the Table is rather small, compared to the Line, and it is situated on each end of the Table. It reads "Don't Pass," "Bar Aces" or "Bar Two Sixes." Both these bets are identical, so it does not matter which you bar. If you go back to the chart, you will note the same percentages for each, except that you are betting the dice lose. *The line is where the Shooter wins,* either by throwing 7 or 11 the first roll, or he gets a Point and makes it before he throws a 7.

## Don't Pass

Don't Pass is a bet that the Line loses. When the Shooter gets a Point and throws a 7 before he makes the Point, the Don't Pass gets paid off.

## Bar Two Aces

Bar Two Aces means this, that on the Come-Out, if a Shooter throws two Aces, as the Bar reads, it is a stand-off or a tie; you neither win nor lose (just a percentage for the House). As small as that percentage is, of throwing two Aces, the House would be giving the percentage to the Player, if there were no Bar; but the House must have a percentage, so the Bar of the two Aces is the House percentage.

Now let's go back to the chart to check the Odds on Points. On the Don't Come, which is just the opposite of the Line (with the exception of the Bar), you lose your money if the Shooter throws 7 or 11, and you win if the Shooter throws Ace Deuce or Deuce Ace or two Sixes (two Aces no bet or a stand off). To break it down according to the Chart, you can lose on 7 or 11.

Ways to throw 7 is 6
Ways to throw 11 is 2

8 ways of losing on Come-Out (Don't Pass).

You can win on Ace Deuce, Deuce Ace and two Sixies (if two Aces are barred):

Ways to throw 3 is 2
Ways to throw 12 is 1

3 ways of winning on the Come-Out if you bet Don't Pass.

Now if the Shooter throws a Point, which will be 4, 5, 6, 8, 9 or 10, ways to throw each Point are:

Number  4      3 ways
Number  5      4 ways
Number  6      5 ways
Number  8      5 ways
Number  9      4 ways
Number 10      3 ways

24 ways to throw a Point.

After the Shooter has a Point, the Odds that he does not make it are as follows:

4—2 to 1 he does not make it.
5—3 to 2 he does not make it.
6—6 to 5 he does not make it.
8—6 to 5 he does not make it.
9—3 to 2 he does not make it.
10—2 to 1 he does not make it.

So you see, once a Shooter makes a Point, the Odds are against his making it. Therefore, this favors the Don't Pass. Yet on the Come-Out you can lose eight ways and win only three. This particular bet of Don't Pass has a very thin margin of percentage in favor of the House. As you know, two Aces is 30 to 1 that the House will lay you, although it is actually 35 to 1 on our chart; yet you do not win your money on the Don't Pass, if two Aces come up. Therefore, up to this point, this is the best bet play for the Player, although it has its drawbacks and is not played by the average Player. The reason is that it is very slow action, with the Player winning an amount equal to that which he puts up; if he doubles up and the dice pass, he loses twice as much money. On the other hand, if a Player has patience and can make the same bet every time, never varying, he has an excellent chance of winning a small amount, depending on his initial investment, over a period of hours. Or, in the parlance of gambling, he can grind out a few dollars only because the percentage involved is so small. However, later I will give you a system on this type of play.

### Don't Come

This bet is identical to Don't Pass only when your bet is placed in this square after the Shooter is shooting for a Point. This is the same as the Come-Out roll in Don't Pass. A Player can place a bet in Don't Come on every roll of the dice. When a Player bets on Don't Come and comes out with a Point, the dealer takes the money and puts it behind the Marker, signifying that the Don't Come bet is against that particular number.

### Come Bet

Like the Don't Come, a Come bet can be placed in this square at any time, regardless of the number the Shooter has as a Point. Only, in this case, it is identical to the Line, or betting that the Shooter makes his first throw a winning 7 or 11, or if a Point, that he makes it. However, in this bet, when placed on a Point, the dealer places the Come bet on the number of the marker. To simplify this bet, if you place a bet on Come, and I place a bet on Don't Come, and the Shooter throws 9, both bets are placed on 9, with the Don't Come bet in back of the 9 and the Come bet on the 9. The action terminates when the Shooter throws either 9 or 7. In such a case, the dealer puts the winning bet back where it was originally placed, paying it off at even money. If he makes the number 9 his Point, the dealer puts the original bet on the Come and pays it off with an equal amount. Whereas he puts the Don't Come money in his rack or vice versa.

It is not advisable to let Don't Pass or Don't Come bets ride, or to bet your original investment along with your profit on the next roll. The reason is simple. If you win a bet and lose the next one, you are out your original investment, so that if every first bet were a winning one and every second bet a losing one, at the end of the play you would have lost every bet. However, I will give you a system on wrong betting.

## System on Wrong Betting

From all the Odds and Percentages, one can readily see that everything is based on the first roll, Odds on the Come-Out favoring 7 or 11 (Line) or a Point. After the Point is obtained, the Odds favor Don't Pass. Now, what Odds do you think that the House would give that the Shooter makes four Passes? The House does not quote any such Odds. Let's try and decipher them for ourselves.

The Odds against 7 coming out are 5 to 1.

The Odds against 4 consecutive 7's are 1296 to 1.

The Odds against 11 coming out are 17 to 1.

The Odds against 4 consecutive 11's are 104,976 to 1.

So you see the Odds are greatly in your favor that the Shooter will not throw four consecutive naturals (that is, 7 or 11). Each Point then reverts to its original Odds; for example, if the Point is 4, the Odds are 2 to 1 he does not make it. If he makes the 4 and comes out on 4 the second time, the Odds remain unchanged, 2 to 1. This applies to all numbers and Odds, as the chart shows.

## Don't Pass System

Always remember that each throw is a new throw, and all percentages and Odds remain the same.

The best wrong system that the writer has ever seen is to start with $100 capital and bet the following way:

1st bet, $5 Don't Come—if he makes it
2nd bet, $10 Don't Come—if he makes it
3rd bet, $20 Don't Come—if he makes it
4th bet, $40 Don't Come—if he makes it
Total Bet $75

With a bet of this type, you are betting $75 to $5 that the Shooter does not make four Passes, whether they be naturals (7 or 11) or Points. This bet is made on every Shooter, and it never varies. No matter which of the first four passes the Shooter misses, you win $5. If ten Shooters in succession make one, two or three passes, you are ahead $50. This system of betting is a slow plodding system. As explained before, a bet on Don't Come at even money without bar favors the Don't Come bet. In other words, when a Player places a bet on the Line, the House bets even money he doesn't make it. The House takes this type of bet up to the limit. However, when you are betting on the Don't Come, the House says two aces are barred, or a stand-off, should the Shooter come out on two aces. As you can see on the Chart, it is 35 to 1 that the Shooter does not throw two aces; and, if he does, you do not lose your money but get a stand-off. However, you will find that these two aces do come up, and sometimes at the wrong time. For example, the Shooter may throw two passes, then throw two aces and then make two passes, which cost you $75. But as the Odds indicate, this is none too frequent. When a Shooter does make four passes, you stop. The reasons for this are numerous. One, first your capital does not warrant going on. Second, as explained above, if a Shooter makes four, heaven only knows how many he can make; and it might take the capital of the Bank of America to keep on playing until he misses.

Always remember each pass is separate and distinct, with the Come Out and the same combinations and percentages against the Shooter, whether it be his first shot with the dice or his tenth pass. My suggestion in playing this system is to set a goal as to what you want or expect. If your investment is $100, as suggested above, play until you double your capital and have $200, and then stop. Play again a few hours later or the next day.

Dice are peculiar and seem to run in cycles. They will miss or Don't Pass for long periods sometimes, and suddenly right about face and pass, until you lose your shirt betting wrong.

# Chapter 16

## Pass System

Betting the Line (or Right), means that you are betting with the Shooter. This bet is even money, with the percentage in favor of the House. As you know from the past paragraph, the winning numbers on the Come Out are 7 and 11. The losing numbers are 2, 3 and 12. There are six ways of throwing 7, two ways of throwing 11, which makes eight possible combinations to win on the Come Out.

1 way of throwing 2 (aces)

2 ways of throwing 3 (ace-deuce, deuce-ace)

1 way of throwing 12 (2-6's)

4 possible ways to lose on the Come Out.

Therefore, there are twelve combinations on the first roll of the dice that terminate the bet on the first roll; eight win and four lose.

Through simple mathematics with 36 combinations—the action of which twelve take place on the first roll—leaving 24 ways to make a Point, so naturally it is a 2 to 1 bet that the Shooter will come out on a Point. Once a Point is obtained, we then think of Odds. If a Shooter has 4 for a Point, the Odds are 2 to 1. Our original Line is at even money, therefore the House percentage on our Line bet is 50 percent, because we bet even money on the Line. As the Odds vary according to the Point obtained, so does the House percentage.

Let's go to the other extreme and select 6 or 8 as a Point. The Odds in favor of the House change. As we know, the Odds on 6 or 8 that the Shooter does not make it are 6 to 5. This is 20 percent in the House's favor. So you see, you must know the Odds, and in betting Right or on the Line (which is the same) on the Point 4, the percentage against the Shooter is

50 percent, while with 6 or 8 the percentage against the Shooter is only 20 percent. The only possible chance that a Right or Line Bettor has to win is to cut down the House's percentage.

How can we cut percentage, when—as previously stated and proved according to our Chart—that percentage always remains the same? Yes, we can cut percentage, not by changing the roll of the dice, but by taking Odds. If this were not permitted, no one but the suckers would bet the Line. With the percentages against the Line, their play would dwindle to nothing, or be overwhelming on the Don't Pass.

To give you an example of this type of play, we must know that the *House permits double Odds*. There is no note, sign or advertisement to this effect around a Crap Table. Why? The House does not want this type of play, as it cuts down their percentage. Yet they must give these Odds to attract the high-rolling gambler, without whose play they could not pay expenses. Let us illustrate with an example.

Take the same Player, same Odds and the same numbers, and let us see how we cut down the percentage in favor of the House. The Shooter places $2 on the Line—4 is the Point (50 percent in favor of the House). The Shooter then places $4 in back of his bet, indicating that he is taking the Odds, which are 2 to 1. Now the Shooter has $2 on the Line at even money on a 4, and $4 behind the Line at 2 to 1. His total investment is $6. If the Shooter makes the 4, he gets paid off $2 even on the Line and $8 behind the Line for the $4 Odds he took on his Point 4. So we again look at percentage. Total investment is $6, total payoff is $10. So far our investment of $6 has picked up $16, which is $10 profit on the bet, so you see we have cut the House's percentage from a $2 Line bet, with 50 percent in favor of the House, to only 20 percent in favor of the House on Point 4.

Now let's take 6 and 8.

With the same bet of $2 on the Line, we take 6 to 5 Odds. Our total bet is $2 and $5, which is $7. If the Point is 6

58

and the Shooter makes it, we get back $2 for our Line bet and $6 for our Odds. The sum total bet is $7 and we get back $8. So you see we are getting 8 to 7 for our total bet, which is roughly 12½ percent in favor of the House, whereas with the same $2 Line bet the Odds were 20 percent in favor of the House. By taking Odds on the 6 we cut down the House's percentage 7½ percent, which mounts up as the game goes on.

In betting the dice Right, it is imperative that we take the Odds. *The COME bet is identical to the Line after the Player has obtained a Point.* It is always advisable to let your Line bet ride for at least two passes. The Odds, because they are at a disadvantage to the House, can be picked up at any time.

Since a Come bet and a Line bet are identical, the Shooter may choose to take several Points and Double Odds on both.

As explained, the Line Point is obtained, which we will call 4. We have bet $2 on the Line and have placed $4 behind the Line at 2 to 1 Odds. We then place $2 on the Come. The Shooter throws 10 for a Point on the Come bet. We take $4 Odds (which is double Odds). Our total investment is $12, $2 on the Line and $4 Odds, $2 on the Come and $4 Odds. If the Shooter throws one or the other, 4 or 10, you win on the roll, plus $2 flat bet and $4 Odds, which are still working for us on the opposite number.

Let's break this down into a simpler and more understandable calculation.

As explained, we have $12 invested, $6 on 4 and $6 on 10. When the Shooter throws 4, the dealer pays off our original Line bet of $2 at even money, and $8 for our $4 invested in taking double Odds. The figures would add up

```
$2 Line bet at even money = $ 4
$4 Double Odds            = $12
                            $16  total
```

So you see we have $4 profit from both our bets on numbers 4 and 10, while our $2 Come bet with $4 double Odds are still working. However, if the Shooter should happen to make the number 10 as well, you then have a sum total of $32 for your original $12 investment.

In referring back to our original chart on Odds, we will find these figures to be facts. There are six ways to make a 7 (which is a loser); there are three ways of making 4. So with six ways of making 10 and 4 combined and six ways of making 7, it is a dead bet that the Shooter will make either 4 or 10 before he makes a 7. Yet the Shooter, with his $12 invested, as shown above, will get $16 in return for his bet, if one or the other Point is made, which changes the Odds from favoring the House to favoring the Shooter, giving the Shooter 25 percent the best of it financially.

All other bets work similarly, with a varying percentage, depending on the numbers. It is well for the Player to work each and every bet out for himself on paper, rather than plunge into a Crap Game and attempt to work it out while playing.

Take a Gambler and see how he would play the game for two passes, making the same $2 bet on the Line.

The Shooter throws 4. He takes the Odds—$4 worth of Odds (double). The Gambler's next move would be to bet $2 on Come. The Shooter throws 6. He takes the Odds, 6 against 5 on the 6. Here the Gambler has two Points, 4 on the Line and 6 on the Come. In the course of rolling, the Shooter throws 6. He wins the Come bet, and is paid off $2 for $2 Come bet and $6 for his Odds. The total invested on the Come bet was $7, and he receives back $15, which is *$8 profit*. The Shooter is still shaking for his Number 4 Point, on which he has an investment of $6 ($2 on the Line and $4 Odds). At this point, if the Shooter fails to make his Number 4 Point, our profit is $2. If he makes 4, then we get paid off—$2 on our Line bet and $8 for $4 Odds. Total bet on the 4 was $6 ($2 on the Line and $4 Odds). He has a total pickup of $16, which gives him a profit of $16 minus his $6, which nets a $10 profit.

60

Let's recap the bets to determine if he missed both the Come bet and the Point and note losses. (see Chart, page 62.)

These figures unquestionably are complicated as you read them, but once you understand them they are very simple. In the course of a Game, one does not attempt to calculate the amount won or lost on each Pass or bet won. The prime object is to cut down the House's percentage against you and give you the greatest amount of profit with the smallest amount of investment.

You often hear of people making ten or twenty Passes with the dice, or even some fantastic number of Passes, or holding the dice for an hour. These cases are rare, but they do happen; and if you are present in the game at that particular time, you will reap a harvest, providing you "know how to bet."

I once saw a man make 22 Passes, and at the end he had won $11. The reason for his small winning was that he would bet $1 on the Line and draw it down after every Pass. Occasionally, he would bet $1 on the Field and lose it.

Always remember, when a Shooter holds the dice for a long period of time, he is making a lot of Come Bets, as well as a lot of Points.

To simplify matters, we will take the case of a man making four Passes, and give you an idea of multiplicity and Odds. In so doing I will pick numbers at random with small bets.

1. Bettor places $2 on Line, throws 4 for a Point, puts $4 behind Line (Odds), makes it. Decides to let $2 Line Bet ride for three Passes.

2. Bets $4 on Line, Point 9, bets $8 Odds, makes it.

3. Bets $8 on Line, Point 10, bets $16 Odds, makes it.

Let us at this point check each of his three bets.

1. To start with, his Line bet was $2, which he lets ride, so the most money he can lose on the Line is $2.

61

Line $2, Point is 4, Odds $ 4 at 2 to 1 — total bet $ 6.  If made, collects  $16
Come $2, Point is 6, Odds $ 5 at 6 to 5 — total bet $ 7.  If made, collects  $15
Total                                                                         $31
  Bet $4        $ 9      $13  Investment is minus  $13
                                      If both are made  $18 profit

Let's change the numbers:
The same Shooter is coming out again, he leaves $4 on the Line (double).
Line $4, Point is 9, Odds $ 8 at 3 to 2 — total bet $12.  If made, collects  $28
Come $2, Point is 5, Odds $ 4 at 3 to 2 — total bet $ 6.  If made, collects  $14
    $6         $12       Investment is minus  $18
                                      If both are made  $24 profit

If the Shooter makes the Point, you must win on the roll, even if he loses the Come Bet. Total invested $18, total pickup $28, profit $10.

If Shooter makes Come and loses on Line, Total pickup  $14
                                    Total invested  $18
                                    Total Loss  $ 4

If the Shooter makes his Line bet, No. 9 which he has $4 on the Line and $8 Odds, then fails to make his No. 5 on the Come bet, it would work out like this:

        $8 Double Odds on No. 9 at 3 to 2 = $20 pick up
        $4 Flat bet at even money       = $ 8 pick up
        Total pick up on Line bet
                    plus Odds = $28 or $16 profit

If the Shooter fails to make the Come bet, which is on No. 5, we would deduct $6, $2 for the flat bet and $4 Double Odds. If this loss of $6 were deducted from our $16 profit we gained from our Line bet, we would then show a profit of $10 from winning our Line bet with Double Odds and losing our Come bet with Double Odds.

His first Point was 4, with $4 behind the Line (or Odds), and he wins $8. (2 to 1)

2. His second Point was 9, with $8 behind the Line (or Odds), and he wins $12. (3 to 2)

3. His third Point was 10, with $16 behind the Line (or Odds), and he wins $32. (2 to 1)

Profit on three Passes was $52 (from Odds only).

On the Line he now has $16 from his original investment of $2, which is a profit of $14.

At this point he has $66 profit. Shall he go on or stop? He decides to go, splitting the Line bet. In other words, leave a little and save a little. By this is meant, put $8 on the Line (which gives us a $6 profit from the original Line bet).

4. Bets $8 on Line, Point 6, bets $20 to $24 at Odds (6 to 5).

At this point, we will stop and analyze where he stands— if he makes it or if he loses.

*Prior to this roll, he has $66 profit.*

4. Bet $8 on the Line, takes $20 Odds, stands to lose $28 on this roll, which will mean that if the Shooter, who has made three Passes and now shooting for the fourth, *fails to make the Point 6,* he will, regardless, have a profit of $38.

If, on the other hand, he makes the Point 6, he will have $16 on the Line and $44 behind the Line, or a

| | |
|---|---|
| Total pickup of | $60 |
| Investment $8 Line Bet $20 Odds | $28 |
| Profit on this one bet | $32 |
| His total profit | $98 |

However, in playing this system, he could have also been playing on the Come and taking the Odds, which, in conjunction with his $98 profit from the Line Bets and Odds, could have won him considerably on the Come bets.

Now, dear reader, you can see by your small investments and large returns, that it does not require one to make those ten or fifteen Passes to win money, and should it happen, which is unusual, you can reap a harvest.

# Chapter 17

## Importance of Odds

This system of Double Odds is not permitted either at the State Line or Las Vegas.

It is obvious I must answer your question, "Why?"

The percentage in favor of the casino is dismissed in the multiplication of Odds and doubling up of bets. Your next question is, "Why then do they permit it in Reno?"

First, they get mostly small Players.

Second, very few Players know of this system.

Third, this type of play shows lots of money on the Table and attracts the Suckers, whose money is a gift. And this group of people makes up 90 percent of the Play.

Most of all, Double Odds attract business, Players.

At one time, the Nevada Club in Reno attempted to attract business by lying Triple Odds, but was soon forced to abandon the idea.

Las Vegas and State Line abandoned Double Odds, because they are much too dangerous for the casino.

In the Wagon Wheel at the State Line, there is a sign over the Crap Table which reads,

>Limit of this Table $400
>
>Single Odds up to $ 200 on $400 no Odds

The above should prove the importance of Odds to the Player.

If you recall, in the first few pages of this book, I referred constantly to percentage, which favor the House. The exact percentage in favor of the House on flat bets Right and Wrong (Line and Don't Pass) is calculated by expert mathematicians as being 1.414 percent against the Shooter. This percentage is very small, but on a continued 24-hour-per-day play, 365 days a year, it amounts to considerable money. However, all money bet on Craps, Eleven, Seven or Doubles, two Treys, Fours, Fives or Deuces, and the Field as well as Six and Eight, runs as high as 20 percent in favor of the House, as I have shown in an earlier paragraph.

It is these bets, and the percentages in favor of the House, that makes the Crap Table so lucrative for the Gambling Casino.

To go on with more detail regarding this game of Crap, you will hear people, who know nothing of the game, give you all sorts of percentages and systems. On the contrary, I have attempted to prove to you in as simple a method as possible, how percentages are arrived at, and how to overcome them, or minimize the percentage against the Player.

My hope is that after reading this far, you are beginning to understand percentage of dice, as well as how to play the game to your advantage. Therefore, I am going into a little more detail that no doubt will puzzle you, if you are a beginner.

For example: the Odds on Number 4 are 2 to 1. The Odds always remain 2 to 1. In other words, if a Shooter has a Point 4 and makes it, and on the very next roll he throws another 4 for his Point, the Odds still remain 2 to 1.

Many people misunderstand this and would attempt to calculate it thusly: the Point 4, 2 to 1 he doesn't make it. If he makes it and comes out on a 4 for a Point, the Odds should be 2 to 1 times 2, which is four times 2, or 8 to 1, which is not so.

Always remember, that once you get a point, the Odds are the same as the chart shows you, regardless of how many times you have had that point and made it.

What confuses some people is that before the Shooter throws the dice, if one were to bet that the Shooter would throw Number 4 four times before throwing a 7, the Odds would be fantastic. Once the Shooter has thrown a number, such as 4, the Odds are as shown on the chart, 2 to 1, that he does not make it before he throws Number 7.

## Field System

I have seen all kinds and types of systems. Just recently, I saw two men playing a system on the Field.

Their system was to stand by and not make a bet until a Field number did not come up for four consecutive rolls of the dice. On the fifth roll, they would place $50 on the Field. If a Field number did not come up, they would follow through by increasing their bet on the next roll to $100. If this failed, their next bet would be $150, and their fourth bet would be $200 (the limit is $200).

Their system was, that percentagewise a Field number should come up within eight rolls.

To those unfamiliar with the Field, if you will refer back to the chapter on the Field, you get a good idea of the percentage on a Field number coming up on each or any roll of the dice.

However, these partners would alternate. When one got tired standing waiting for the Field number that failed to show up within the four rolls to place the system in vogue, the other would take his place.

Don't forget that two aces pay double in the Field, and that two sixes pay triple.

However, after a 24-hour play with this system they were $4,000 ahead. Yes, dear reader, they had plenty of capital to start the playoff of the system. This is a poor system and by no means advocated by the author.

Some people take Six and Eight and use a progression system by doubling up on each roll until the number is finally rolled—another poor system.

## Place Betting

This type of betting is very important to this author. At no time has he ever seen in writing an explanation of Place Betting. The reason for this is that the percentage in favor of the House is so minute that they avoid any and all explanations of this method of betting. Place Betting is designed exclusively to attract Players and Gamblers who know what it it all about and understand percentages thoroughly and are attracted to play because of the bargain rates. The minimum Place Bet that is permitted is $5. This is how it works.

A Player at any time can select his own Number and give the Dealer his $5 to place on the Number of his choice. This bet can be placed at any time, and it can be withdrawn at any time.

For example, if he selects Number 4, he gives the Dealer $5, which the Dealer places on 4 the same as he would on a Come Bet. Of the $5 bet, $1 would be a Flat Bet of even money and $4 would be at the correct Odds of 2 to 1, which are the Odds on 4. If the Shooter should throw Number 7, he naturally loses his $5 Place Bet, just as he would a Come Bet. If the Shooter throws 4, he will receive back $14 for his $5 bet.

The payoff would be on this basis: $1 even money and $4 at 2 to 1, which would give him a payoff of $14.

Numbers such as 4, 5, 9 and 10, when a $5 Place Bet is made, are paid off at the ratio of $1 Flat Bet and the correct Odds of the number selected.

In the case of 4 and 10, it would be $1 Flat Bet and 2 to 1 for the remaining $4.

In the case of 5 and 9, it would be $1 Flat Bet and 3 to 2 on the remaining $4.

In the case of 6 and 8, there is a slight deviation. The Place Bet, instead of being $5 minimum is $6 minimum. The reason for this is because of the Odds. So with the $6 Place Bet on 6 and 8, it would be $1 Flat Bet and the correct Odds of 6 to 5 for the remaining $5.

I have told you that this Place Bet was designed to attract gamblers and those that know what it is all about, and the bargain rates of minimized percentage. So to recapitulate, let us figure roughly the percentage in favor of the House, plus the bargain rate that is offered.

The normal House percentage on a Flat Bet or Line Bet is 1.414 percent in favor of the House, which normally on a $5 bet would be the equivalent to 7¢ for a $5 bet. As I have explained to you previously, the correct Odds offer no percentages whatsoever either in favor of the House or the Player. In other words, the correct Odds on Number 4 are 2 to 1, but the House would not stand by and lay you 2 to 1 on a 4 or a 10 without a Flat Bet, because there would be no percentage for the House.

I also explained in previous chapters the importance of Double Odds, which is only permitted in Reno, Nevada, but is not acceptable in Las Vegas, because there is no percentage in it for the House.

You can now see that in a Place Bet, the only percentage that the House has is on a Flat bet of $1, and yet they are laying you quadruple. This is the highest Odds that the House lays on any Point.

If the House did not receive the $1 Flat Bet, they would be playing a dead-even game with no percentage at all.

Let us analyze how it works, so that we can more clearly understand Place Betting.

If, for example, we Placed Number 5, we have $1 Flat Bet and $4 at Double Odds. If the Shooter makes the Number 5, our payoff would be $1 at even money and $6 to $4 (correct Odds on 5 are 3 to 2), therefore, our total return would be $12.

If, on the other hand, the casino (which is not permitted) would lay the correct Odds on the Point 5 for a $5 Bet, the correct payoff would be $7.50 to $5 or a gross return of $12.50. This is a no-percentage type of bet. The sum total difference would be 50¢. This difference is caused by the $1 Flat Bet, if it were utilized as an Odds Bet, would get the Player back $2.50 instead of $2.

However, Place Betting has many advantages. First, you can select your own Place number; second, as many of them as you so desire; and third, you can put them on at any time or take them down at any time.

From the above Place Betting you readily see that the House is actually laying you 9 to 5 on the point 4 or 7 to 6 on numbers 6 and 8.

A common system or pattern of play is as follows:

Bet $5 on the Line, always letting your bet ride for at least two Passes.

Take Double Odds on all Points and make a Place Bet equal to your Odds behind the Line.

For detailed explanation, we will break this down and start a Play:

We bet $5 on the Line.

If a Shooter throws 7 or 11, we win and let the $10 go.

If the Shooter throws a Crap (two 6s, two aces or Ace Deuce) we lose.

We then start all over, betting $5 on the Line.

No doubt, after reading this far, you realize that on the Come out you can win eight ways, that is, with a 7, which is six ways, and with an 11, which is two ways. On the other hand, you can lose four ways on the Come out, (two 6s, two Aces, Deuce Ace or Ace Deuce). Therefore, eight ways to win and four ways to lose on the Come out will leave a balance of 24 ways to make a Point or Number not in the win or lose column. It is, as previously explained, because of these circumstances, that the House has the advantage of percentage in their favor, which amounts to 1.414 percent. It is this percentage that we are trying to eradicate, minimize and change to favor us instead of the House.

Therefore, we will skip over the one-roll win or lose as explained above and go on to the Points, of which there are 24 possible combinations, furthermore eliminating the House percentage to little or nothing.

Now to continue with our Play betting $5 on the Line.

The Shooter throws 9 for his Point.

We take Double Odds behind the Line, which is $15 to $10. Also we place number 5 for $10 (refer to Place Betting).

At this point, we must analyze two things, first, the amount of money invested and second, the possibilities of winning.

Amount of money invested         $ 5 on the Line
        Double Odds                 $10
        Total                     $15

Total $10 Place Bet on Number 5. Total amount invested, $25.

As you know, the Shooter either throws 9 and wins or 7 and loses. We also have $10 Place Bet on 5, whereby the Shooter either throws 5 and wins the Place Bet, or throws 7 and loses.

As the dice are continued to be thrown, we conclude our percentage. There are six ways to throw 7, four ways to throw 9, and also four ways to throw 5, so the possibilities of winning one of the two bets is 8 to 6 in our favor.

Now that we have the pattern of our play mapped out, we will continue.

Naturally, as you know, if the Shooter throws a 7 before either 5 or 9, we lose our total investment of $25.

On the other hand, for example, if the Shooter throws 9, which is the Point, what do we get for our $25 invested?

We win—$ 5 on the Line
           $15 for our $10 Double Odds on 9

We receive a total (including our own money) of
           $10 on the Line,
           $25 Behind the Line
           $35

We take down our $10, which we placed on 5, so our capital is $45 for the $25 invested.

Now, let us assume that the Shooter throws 5 in the course of his shooting before he throws either 7 or 9. (Always bear in mind that we have a total of $25 bet on this Shooter, and we have two Points—5 and 9).

If the Shooter throws 5, we win our Place Bet and draw it all down, which amounts to $24 ($10 Place Bet is figured, $2 even and $12 to $8 Odds, which is $14 profit to our $10 invested, and by drawing it all down we have $24). Our original investment was $25, and we now have $24 returned, so our present investment is now $1.

For this $1, we have a $5 Line Bet and $10 Odds. If the Shooter makes his Point 9, we get back $10 on the Line and $25 behind the Line, which is our Line bet and Odds included, or a sum total of $35. At this moment we now have $35 plus $24, which is $59, minus our investment of $25, a $34 profit.

If these figures appear complicated to you, we will try to approach the subject from another angle to help clarify this method.

As you know, all Odds are based on the frequency of occurrence of Number 7, which is the basis of the entire game of Crap. Therefore, the Odds on any Point are six to the number of ways the other Point can be made. For example:

There are three ways to make Number 4

There are six ways to make Number 7

Thus the odds are 3 to 6 or 2 to 1. The same applies to Number 10. If two men are rolling a pair of dice indefinitely and one took Number 7 and the other man was allowed two numbers, 4 and 10, it would be a dead-even bet. Neither man would have any percentage or advantage. Why? There are three ways to make 4 and three ways to make 10, or six ways to make either one or the other. On the other hand, there are six ways to make 7. Therefore, it is six against six or an even bet, but according to this method of play, by the manipulation of money, you reverse a dead-even bet to a profit in your favor.

Now I will repeat the previous Play, using the numbers 4 and 10.

As you know, your original bet of $5 on the Line has the possibilities of winning eight ways and losing four, so therefore your initial bet on the first roll is 2 to 1; you win it rather than lose it on the Come out, which naturally excludes Points. If you included Points, it is 2 to 1 that you throw a Point rather than a natural or crap.

71

To go on with our Play with a $5 Flat Bet, the Shooter throws 4 for his Point; we bet $10 Odds and a $10 Place Bet on Number 10. Again we have a total investment of $25. *It is an even bet* that the Shooter will throw 4 or 10 as against 7.

Let us assume that the Shooter throws 10. We get $28 by drawing down our entire Place Bet on 10. As our original bet on both 4 and 10 was a total of $25, we now have a $3 profit on a $25 investment, yet we have $15 bet on Number 4, which does not cost us anything. If perchance the Shooter throws his 4, we then get $10 on the Line and $30 behind the Line or a total draw down of $40, plus the $28 we got on the Place Bet on 10, a total of $68 for making 4 and 10. In other words, we make a profit on an even bet.

Take 6 and 8. It is 10 to 6 Odds that the Shooter will throw either 6 or 8 before he throws 7. The only difference on the 6 and 8 play, from that described above on the other numbers, is on the Place Bet. On these two numbers you must put $12 Place, so therefore your initial investment is $27 instead of $25.

If 8 is the Point, you put $12 Place Bet on 6. If he makes the 6, you get back $26 on a investment of $27. In other words, after the Shooter makes the 6, your total investment is $1. Yet you have $5 on the Line and taking $10 Odds, all for but $1. If he makes his Point 8, you collect $32 for your $1 investment.

Let's assume that the Shooter makes his Point first. We get $5 Line Bet at even money, plus $12 Odds or a total payoff of $32, and we withdraw our Place Bet of $12 on Number 6, so we then have a total of $32 plus $12, or $44 for our investment of $27, or $17 profit.

## Shooting for the Second Pass

I advise a $10 Line Bet, Double Odds and the Place Bet on the opposite number equal to the Odds which are doubled, as explained above.

72

The procedure from here on, as long as the Shooter is Passing, is the $10 Line Bet, Odds, and so on. However, if you hit a "hot hand," with Pass after Pass being made and you are well ahead, you can, at your discretion, up the Line Bet, but never bet more on the Line than you can afford to take *DOUBLE ODDS* on the Point, and an equal amount of your Odds as a Place Bet on the opposite number.

From this type of Play, the conclusion is this: eight ways to win on the Come out; four ways to lose on the Come out.

If the Shooter throws a Point, 5 or 9, being that we have both numbers, the Odds are 8 to 6 that he makes either 5 or 9 before he throws a 7. The Odds being 3 to 2 on Number 5 and 3 to 2 on Number 9, which equals eight ways (4 ways to make Number 5, and 4 ways to make Number 9, which equals 8 ways to throw either one or the other), with but six ways to make Number 7 the loser.

With Numbers 4 and 10, it's 6 to 6 or even money that he makes either one of these numbers before he throws 7.

With Numbers 6 and 8, it is 10 to 6 that he throws either 6 or 8 before he throws a 7.

Now you can readily see from the figures quoted that every Point that the Shooter throws by combining it with the Place Bet, you have a better than even bet against the 7.

In the case of Numbers 10 and 4, it is even against 7, and in the case of Numbers 6 and 8, you have 10 to 6 in your favor, and in the case of numbers 9 and 5, you have 8 to 6 also in your favor.

You will also note that if the Place Bet is made and the Line Bet is lost, the profit and loss is very trivial, but if the Line Bet is made, the profit skyrockets for the amount of money invested.

This type of play is very common and used by many gamblers, but the fact that you lose percentagewise is the payoff of your Place Bet.

The complication rests not with the Line Bet and the Double Odds, which are correct, but with the Place Bet.

To explain in detail, I refer you to the best system in a

later chapter, but at the moment, to explain the percentage difference of the Place Bet, I will take $5 on the Line and $10 Double Odds on No. 9, $10 Place on No. 5. On both 9 and 5, the correct odds are identical—6 to 4.

The payoff on the Place Bet is your loss or increased house percentage because you are laying $2 even on No. 5 in order to get $12 to $8. The Odds are okay, but the $2 even on 5 is big percentage against you. To get a correct even break in percentage, you should get $3 to $2 on your flat bet and $12 to $8 on your odds. The result is, you are losing $1 in this case on the Point No. 5. Therefore, as small as it seems, $1 on a $10 investment is 10 per cent against you, much too much against you. Spend time studying the best system.

# Chapter 18

## Place Bets vs. Come Bets

This is a controversial subject among shrewd gamblers, yet very few explain it satisfactorily, and the majority do not understand it at all. To the average Player, this is one of the mysteries of the Game.

To simplify the difference between these two bets, we must realize the factor of percentage, which is emphasized throughout this book.

We have definitely established and accepted that the percentage in favor of the House on a Flat Bet or Line Bet is 1.41 per cent, or in simple transition, 7¢ on every $5 bet on the Line. We have also explained in a previous paragraph on Come Betting that the Line Bet and the Come Bet are identical in every respect. That is, you win and lose on the Come Bet just as you do on the Line. The only difference is that, on the first throw of the Dice, the wager is placed on the Line, and action is taken according to what the Shooter throws. If a Point is thrown, that is the number that your money is riding on, and if he makes his point you win. If he throws 7, you lose.

So it is with the Come Bet. The only difference is that after having thrown a Point, you can make a bet on the Come. If the Shooter throws another Point, the Come money is placed on that number, so as a result you then have two different numbers. You can continue these Come Bets until you have all the numbers covered and take Odds on each number. Occasionally the Shooter will throw his Line Point, which is paid off, having no effect on the Come Bets.

As you know, odds are optional. You can put them on or

take them off at will, as Odds are just courtesy of the House and they receive no percentage.

Many times after the Line number is made, and the Shooter is coming out for a new Point, the Player can draw down his Odds or tell the Dealer they are off for this roll.

This is very common, because if the Shooter throws 7 on his first throw, you win the Line Bet, but lose your Come Bets, saving the Odds if you withdrew them on this first throw. Usually a sharp Player bets enough on the Line to save his Come Bets, in case the Shooter throws 7 on his first roll.

To explain this Point, if you have two Come Bets at $5 each and Double Odds, you would call off your Odds and bet at least $10 on the Line, so the result would be, if the Shooter comes out with 7, you break even. That is, you lose your two $5 Come Bets, which is $10, and you win $10 on the Line. So you are even on this roll.

Come Betting is very essential in playing the game correctly. The result is you have several Points instead of one and have taken full advantage of Double Odds. The point I wish to emphasize in Come Betting, on every $5 Come Bet you make, that you are paying 7¢, and the Odds are free, that is, no percentage. So if you have two Come Bets of $5 each and $10 Double Odds on each, you are actually paying a 14¢ house percentage on a $30 bet, with the opportunity of winning one or the other, and in so doing actually winning money, even though the Shooter fails to make the second Come number.

A Come Bet has nothing whatsoever to do with the Line Bet. It is actually trying to get another Point, with the possibilities of winning on the first roll (8 possible ways) or losing (4 possible ways).

76

|  | Place Bet | | | | Come Bet | |
| --- | Amount bet as Place Bet | Odds obtained on Place Bet | Total Amount of Payoff, including $15 bet | Correct Odds | $5 on Come after Point is rolled $10 Odds which is Double Odds | Total Amount of Payoff, including $5 plus Odds |
| --- | --- | --- | --- | --- | --- | --- |
| Number 4 | $15 | 9/5 | $42 | 2—1 | $5 + $10 odds | $40 |
| " 5 | $15 | 7/5 | $36 | 3/2 | $5 + $10 odds | $35 |
| " 6 | $18 | 7/6 | $39 | 6/5 | $5 + $10 odds | $32 |
| " 8 | $18 | 7/6 | $39 | 6/5 | $5 + $10 odds | $32 |
| " 9 | $15 | 7/5 | $36 | 3/2 | $5 + $10 odds | $35 |
| " 10 | $15 | 9/5 | $42 | 2—1 | $5 + $10 odds | $40 |

Minimum Place Bet is $5 except in the case of 6 and 8 which is $6.

Minimum Come Bet is $1 (Most Tables).

On this Chart we use $15 as a Place Bet and $5 as a Come Bet with $10 Double Odds, thus making our investment equal on both Come and Place Bets for comparison.

It would appear from a quick glance at the above chart that, with an equal amount of money invested, the Player would receive a greater return from the Place Betting than he would from an equal amount invested on a Come Bet. Untrue.

The Place Bettor bets $15 on the number of his choice. If 7 is thrown the next roll, he loses $15 on the Place Bet, whereas in the case of the Come Bettor, he has only $5 invested, and if the Shooter throws 7 the next roll he wins $5. The difference is the Place Bettor lost $15, whereas the Come Bettor won $5.

77

# Chapter 19

## The Place Bet

As shown on Chart, page 77, you will note that the House will pay you, for example, 9 to 5 on No. 4 or 10. The true Odds on 4 and 10 are 2 to 1, but by Place Betting 4 or 10, they calculate it as $1 Flat Bet or even money, and $4 Odds at 2 to 1, thus giving a return profit of $9 for $5 bet. In other words, you are paid $1 short on $10 payoff, or a 10 percent profit for the House, which is quite a percentage.

To compare the Come Bets with Place Bets, you can actually win eight ways on the Come out first roll of Come Bet (seven or eleven) or lose four ways (crap, ace deuce, two aces, two sixes or deuce ace). Whereas with the Place Bet, you can lose your bet on the first roll six ways (throwing seven), and the only way you can win is for the Shooter to throw the number *you* selected to Place Bet your money. Yet after the first roll, you can win your Come Bet if the Shooter throws the number that your Come Bet is on, the same as the Place Bet.

Therefore, comparing the Place Bet and the Come Bet:

1. You win on both Place or Come Bet, if the number is thrown before 7.
2. On the Come Bet you win if the Shooter throws 7 or 11 on the first roll, or lose if he throws crap.
3. You lose your Place Bet, if the Shooter throws 7 the first roll.

Breaking it down, the difference is, you can win on your Come Bet on the first roll eight ways and lose four ways.

With a Place Bet, you can lose six ways on the first roll, and can only win by throwing the number you have your Place Bet on.

The big difference is, in a Place Bet your odds are included in the bet, whereas with a Come Bet you place your odds *after* you have a number.

After studying the Chart, you will note the Odds that the House is laying you on a Place Bet as well as the correct Odds which they lay you on your Come Bet.

To give perhaps a clearer picture of the difference between Place Bet and Come Bet, we will illustrate a Play.

Shooter bets $5 on the Line. The Point is 10. He takes double odds behind his Line Bet, which is $10. Now, shall he make a Come Bet or a Place Bet?

If he makes a Place Bet he puts $15 on any number. Usually when the Line Point is 10, the Player selects the opposite number, which in this case is 4. If the Shooter comes out with a 7 he loses his line bet of $5 with $10 odds, plus his Place Bet of $15, which is $30 total. Had the Shooter decided to make a Come Bet instead of the Place Bet, here is his procedure:

Bet $5 on the Come, just as he did on the Line. The Shooter, as above, comes out with 7. He wins his Come Bet and loses his Line Bet. His total investment of $5 on the Line and $10 Odds is lost ($15 in all), but he wins $5 on his Come Bet. Therefore, by making the Come Bet, he actually lost $10, whereas by making the Place Bet, he lost $30.

Another Play that is common is to Place all numbers—4, 5, 6, 8, 9, 10. As we know, the minimum Place is $5, except on 6 and 8, which is $6. The reason is to avoid delaying the game by paying off in small change. So this bet would look like this (exclusive of Line bet):

No.  4 — $ 5
No.  5 — $ 5
No.  6 — $ 6
No.  8 — $ 6
No.  9 — $ 5
No. 10 — $ 5
Total — $32

If the Shooter throws a 7, all is lost (six Place Bets of $32 plus the Line Bet). However, if you get a long roll with plenty of numbers, you do well.

One thing the Bettor of this type must take into consideration is that you should average throwing a 7 every fifth roll (36 combinations, 6 ways of making 7); 6 subtracted from 36 equals 30, divide 6 into 30, which is 5, therefore, every fifth roll should average a 7.

Always remember, in betting Come Bets, you win the last bet you make, if the Shooter throws 7.

There is but one point that I must emphasize now, and this is the argument used by every Place Bettor. That is, in a Come Bet you must make the number twice, while in the Place Bet you make it but once.

To clear this point, we repeat, there are 36 combinations on dice, and who are you to pick the number that is coming up next? Every roll of the dice is a new roll, regardless of what was thrown the previous roll; therefore, this roll and each roll thereafter are all based on the calculated percentage of the 36 combinations that are possible on each and every roll.

I have seen a Shooter throw a half dozen 4's and 10's before ever throwing a 6 or 8. Dice frequently run in cycles.

To conclude this discussion of Place Bets vs. Come Bets, percentage favors Come Bets.

You can lose more money making Place Bets than you can Come Bets, and make just about as much with one as the other in a long roll.

### Hedging System

The Hedging System is one where you bet on Don't Pass, and once the Shooter gets his Point you make a Place Bet on the same number. This is what is called Hedging.

If the Player misses his Point, you break even. If the Player makes his Point, you win. In other words, you are betting both Right and Wrong on the same Point, the difference

80

being the Odds which you receive on the Place Bet.

To start with, as we know, there are 24 ways for the Shooter to obtain a Point on the first roll, so it is 2 to 1 that the Shooter will throw a Point rather than a winning or losing number on the first roll.

The Hedge Bettor starts out by putting $10 on the Don't Pass. The Shooter throws, for example, either 4 or 10, which is his Point. He then bets $10 on a Place Bet same number. If the Shooter misses his Point, the Don't Pass wins and he gets back $20 for his Don't Pass bet, and he loses his Place Bet, thus breaking even on the Don't Come and Place Bet, as his total investment was $20.

If the Shooter make his Point, which is 4 or 10, he loses his $10 on Don't Pass, and he wins his Place Bet. His payoff would be $28. Deduct the $20 invested, and he has a profit of $8.

Suppose his point were 5 or 9, $10 on Don't Pass, $10 Place Bet, with a total of $20 invested. If the Shooter fails to make his Point, he again receives back $20 sum total invested, with no profit and no loss. If the Shooter makes his Point, his Place Bet pays off at $24, with a profit of $4.

In 6 and 8 there is a slight difference. He puts up $10 on the Don't Pass and $12 on the Place Bet, a total of $22. If he fails to make his Point, his return is but $20 and he loses $2.

If the Shooter makes his Point, he gets back $26 on his Place Bet, minus the $22 that he has invested, which leaves him a profit of $4.

If you are playing this type of system, you must go back to the system of Don't Pass and progress your bet for four Passes, and do likewise on the Place Bet.

This Hedging method of play is uncommon and *not good*, but an explanation of its broadens your knowledge and scope to understand the system of play that this author will advocate in the next chapter.

# Chapter 20

## Best System

Up until now, we have continually impressed upon you the word Percentage. We have also shown you practically every system of Play, and attempted to show you the Percentage that the casino obtains from each and every Play, and how it operates. Any other types of systems that you might attempt to devise are merely derivatives of those already explained. To explain the only system of Play that this author advocates, we will start by saying it is a Right Betting System.

We start, as aforementioned, with $200 capital for each Play, with cardinal principles, as set forth in an earlier chapter.

First, before we start our Play, or should I say Dive, we must look to see if there is water in the pool, before we jump. By this I mean, look around the casino, select a Crap Table that has plenty of Players, each Player having considerable money in front of him. This means that the dice are passing at this table. We start our Play by buying $100 worth of chips. We bet $5 on the Line; if the Shooter throws a natural, we let the $10 ride. If the Shooter throws a Crap, we bet another $5 on the Line. However, it is most likely that the Shooter will throw a Point. We then take Double Odds on the Point. We also bet $5 on Come and take double odds on that Point. If a Natural or Crap is thrown, we proceed as we did on our Line Bet.

Assuming that we have Two Points, one on the Line and one on the Come, our total investment would be like this —$5 on the Line, plus $10 Double Odds, or a total of $15 bet on the Line Point.

On the Come Bet, we have a similar situation—$5 Come Bet, $10 Double Odds, which also equals $15. Therefore, our

Line Bet and our Come Bet, including Odds, would total $30. Let us recapitulate and see where we stand, and if we have made a good investment. As we know, when we put our first $5 on the Line, there were twelve ways of winning or losing on the first roll; eight ways to win, that is by throwing either 7 or 11, or losing four ways in case of a Crap, two Aces, two 6's, Ace Deuce or Deuce Ace, yet 24 ways of throwing a Point. To clear things up at this point, it is 2 to 1 we win rather than lose on the first roll action. Yet it is 2 to 1 that we throw a Point rather than get a first roll action play (a Natural or Crap). So for simplicity, we select a Point for the first roll, let us say 9, and for our Come Bet we select No. 5.

We have $30 invested, as explained, and we have two Points, 9 on the Line and 5 on the Come Bet. We can either lose both bets, win both bets or win one and lose one. Nothing else can happen at this point.

If we lose both bets, our total loss is $30. If we win one and lose one, Odds being identical on 9 or 5, our payoff would be $5 even, plus $15 to $10 on our Odds, or a total payoff of $35, or $5 profit. If we win both, our total payoff would be $70, or a $40 profit.

Different Points, as I have shown you in previous chapters, vary the payoff according to the Odds on the number thrown. To follow through on our above illustration, our possibility of winning one or the other of our bets on 9 and 5 would work out like this.

There are four ways to make 9 and four ways to make 5. Combined, we have eight possible ways of winning, whereas to lose, the Shooter must throw 7, which has six possible ways of our losing our bets. Therefore, the Odds are 8 to 6 that we win one or the other of our bets.

Each Point Number on the dice can be worked out in a similar manner, as long as you have a Line Bet and a Come Bet. Percentage will favor you making one or the other before throwing the dreaded 7. If the Player makes the Line Bet, I advocate letting the $10 ride on the Line and taking

Double Odds, also a $10 Come Bet with Double Odds. It is only when I am well ahead and betting on a lucky Shooter, that I up my bets into the $20 bracket, but I always follow through by taking Double Odds. At this point I am sure that there are several questions you wish to ask.

First, How about this Percentage business? Answer: This in the lowest Percentage gamble that you can get in any Bank Gambling in a Crap Game. As I showed you previously, the Percentage against the Player betting the Dice Right or on the Line is 1.41 percent in favor of the House. I also proved to you that lying or taking the correct odds is no percentage against the Player or in favor of the House. *It is a dead-even bet.* Now to analyze our bets as quoted above both Line and Come Bet.

We are in round figures paying 7¢ on our Line Bet (1.41 percent of $5). We are also paying 7¢ on our Come Bet (1.41 percent of $5). On our $10 Odds on the Line we are paying nothing. On our $10 Odds on our Come Bet we are paying nothing. Therefore, for our combined bet of $30 (both Line and Come with Odds), we are paying exactly 14¢, which is less than .05 percent on the entire amount wagered. This is the answer to the Great Percentage Problem.

On such a small percentage, a gambling casino cannot operate and be successful. It is only by the foolish high percentage plays that the suckers make, as I have shown you in earlier chapters, that make the Crap Game such a lucrative business for the casinos.

The over-all percentage of money bet on a Crap Table in these casinos runs from 10 to 15 percent every time the dice are rolled. Watch sometime and figure for yourself, if you got 15 percent of the several hundred dollars bet on each roll of the dice, how you would end up at the conclusion of a day's play.

Why did you go to a crowded Table to start with? Answer: Simple, the dice are passing, and everyone is winning, and being a Right Bettor, I too want to win.

Why do you limit your first Play to $200 and then quit

when you know you are going to play more? Answer: Dice are very fickle, they may Pass and Pass with utter disregard for percentage, whereas on the other hand they may miss hours on end with the same disregard for percentage, and only he who is bullheaded will stand losing his entire bankroll in hopes that they will change before he goes broke. Bear in mind, Percentage is based on the long pull, whereby the happy medium prevails, and the Percentage balance is reached.

When the dice are Passing, get as much as you can as fast as you can, because they may change any moment.

It is for this reason that I have put a Stop Loss on your capital, and for the same reason, advocate playing on while you are winning, and, as well, put a stop loss on how much of your winnings you can lose back when things change, leaving you with a substantial profit.

In conclusion, I would like to bring many a gambler's experience to your attention.

To start with, each throw of the dice has the same percentage, whether it be the first or the 21st. By that is meant, if a 7 is thrown on the first roll, the same percentage prevails for the next roll. Or better, if a Shooter has Number 4 for a Point and makes it (which is making two fours before a 7) and then comes out with a 4 for his next Point, the Odds are identical, that is, 2 to 1. You do not look at it as some people would, that the Shooter, to make his Point the second time would be actually making four 4's before throwing one 7. The old saying among the gamblers is, "The dice have no memory or enemies."

Always remember, dice, for some unknown reason, run in cycles, and when they do, percentages mean nothing. Just recently I heard of a man making 21 Passes in the Mapes Hotel. Yet a few months ago, when I was in Reno, someone at the Shriners Convention made 33 Passes at the Riverside Hotel. If several good gamblers were present, betting the dice right during that run, the House would be compelled to close the game because they would run out of money. These, of course, are unusual circumstances.

The average person familiar with the game can walk up to a table and without a word from anyone tell you whether the dice are Passing or not. How? Very simple.

If the dice are Passing, the table is crowded, and all the Right Players have stacks of silver or chips in front of them. If the dice are missing, all the Wrong Bettors are winning, and can be noted by the stack of chips they have, whereas the Line Bettors are all losing and short of money. This condition is also very prominent, if it has continued for some time because the crowd playing has thinned out considerably. If the crowd dwindles to just a few Players, it then becomes necesary for the House to put in Shills to keep the game going.

Dice frequently "chop," as they say; make one Pass, lose, then two Passes and lose. In other words, the majority of people bet the dice Right, or should I say on the Line, and the only way you can make any money to amount to anything on a small investment is to let it ride or, better, Double Up. So you see, if the dice are chopping, the Line Bettor loses his money, because he is letting it ride. Yet the same Player letting his money ride, doubles his investment after every Pass, and if he started with one dollar on the Line and let it ride for three Passes, he has $8. Yet many people will, after the Shooter has made two Passes, switch the bet to Wrong. How ridiculous, you are trying to outguess the dice, and usually end up by jumping the wrong way. Who is to say to a newcomer in a game, "Don't bet on the Line, he has already made five Passes." To the normal individual, this means this Shooter is lucky. Always follow the lucky man. As I have repeatedly said, "Luck overcomes all percentages."

Another point to call to your attention, is that many people by nature are lucky, while others are unlucky. You will see this at almost any table; a few make Passes every time they pick up the dice.

Always remember that the House is continually picking up the sucker bets, namely Field, 6 and 8, 11, Crap or a specific crap, as well as doubles (two 3's and so on). This tremendous percentage in favor of the House, with these sucker plays, throughout a normal day, more than pays all expenses.

So, dear reader, to shoot crap you must play where there is the least percentage against you, and in betting the Line, take the Odds (double) and let your money ride at least twice. Always remember that you limit yourself to the amount you lose, and have not limited yourself to the amount you can win. If you do have a streak of good luck during the course of the play, you end up winning.

In conclusion, after attempting to emphasize the factors of percentages and luck throughout this thesis, I would like to tell you a story that is authentic.

On a cold wintry December night in Reno, Nevada, in 1937, a man down on his uppers, cold and hungry, decided to go in to Harold's Club and get out of the snow and cold. As he stepped through the door, he found a nickel on the floor. Confronted with a slot machine, he unconsciously put the nickel in the slot and pulled the handle. Much to his amazement several nickels came through.

He continued to play and finally hit a Jackpot. Being overcome by his good fortune, he moved on to the dime slot machine, where his luck continued. With capital and good luck he decided to shoot crap, which is faster and affords a greater opportunity for wealth and good fortune, while his luck was running. Here again his lucky streak continued. People gathered around in the wee hours of the morning, watching the "high roller" in tattered clothes rake in the money.

As the dice rolled on and dawn approached, he was $7,000 ahead—wealth and fortune for the man who had neither lodging nor the price of a cup of coffee to keep him warm. Was he satisfied? Did he quit, to live a life of luxury that to him was but a myth? No, he continued on.

As the sun's rays trickled through the grey dawn, our friend's last chip was stacked in the dealer's rack. He slowly headed for the door, tightening up his belt and fastening his coat to face again the cold winter's chill, as penniless as he was on his arrival. This, dear reader, was a gambler who disregarded Percentage.

Never continue indefinitely. Good judgment is permanent, and a necessary factor in everything we do, even shooting Crap.

The majority of people gamble to lose. This sounds like a ridiculous statement, but in about 95 percent of these cases, it is a true statement. Aside from being true, it is very simple to explain; as a matter of fact, you can stand around any casino or any gambling game, and see it happen continuously. Yes, if you told this to any of the thousands of players who go to these places to gamble, they would look at you with amazement. What actually happens is this.

The average player goes to Reno or Las Vegas with a limited amount of money but with high aspirations of winning. Say, for example, he has $50. He plays and wins $100. He then has $150, more than double his original investment. Does he quit? No. Why? Because he has money and came to lose. The result is he continues to play. Naturally, percentage eats up his capital, and finally he is broke. His next move is to bemoan his bad luck and seek a friend from whom he can borrow, or write a check, hoping to win back his original $50 plus his $100 profit. If he is successful, will he quit? No, because he knows that he is lucky and must continue on until he is broke.

Few people ever learn to quit with a profit, or to take a small loss, when they have plenty of money in their pocket. Only seasoned gamblers know these things and follow them. Anytime you double your money, you have made a profitable investment. All the fantastic stories that you read about big winnings in the Crap game are true, but you must realize that the investment or risk is also large.

For example, you have read about Harold Smith winning twenty or thirty thousand in one play. Very simple. He bets perhaps $500 on the line and takes $1000 odds (double); if the Point were 4, he would win $2,500 on this one Point.

88

He will stay and lose $20,000 or win $20,000. When he does, he quits. Compare this with the player who started with $50 and ran it up to $150, but stayed with it and went broke. He expects the impossible with an utter disregard for percentage.

A simple chart to follow: (total investment 40 times initial line bet)

| Investment | Starting Line Bet | Profit anticipated |
|---|---|---|
| $40 | $1 (plus double odds) | $40 |
| 200 | 5 | 200 |
| 400 | 10 | 400 |
| 4,000 | 100 | 4,000 |
| 20,000 | 500 | 20,000 |

Your initial investment covers your anticipated profit.

However, if the dice are "hot" and are continuing to pass, and you have passed your anticipated profit, take your profit out of the game along with your original investment and continue to play until the dice change. Don't quit while you are winning, but don't lose back your capital and profit.

Occasionally, dice go "crazy," and make pass after pass beyond one's fondest expectations. If you are in it, don't quit, but don't lose your original investment and profit, once you have accomplished your goal. On the other hand, take all you can get, because this is a rare situation. Win as much as you can, but don't lose back what you have, after you have closed the book on this day's play.

How many times has it happened to you, and how many times have you heard the same story, "I was a big winner, but blew it all back."

These are the people, about 95 percent of the players, who came to lose.

## Conclusion

In conclusion, let us take a page from the book of the greatest "Gambling Institution" of all—the Stock Market.

You invest your money on a calculated percentage of risk with the anticipation of profit, knowing full well of the possibilities of losing part or all of your investment. Stock market investors are composed of some of our most educated intellectuals in the world. What they do, after they have obtained a suitable profit of say 50 to 100% on their investment, is put a "stop loss order" with the broker to sell if the stock drops to a certain level. Thus they are assured of a profit on their investment. On the other hand, if the stock continues on an upward trend, they continue to increase their profit and from time to time move up the "stop loss order," always being assured of a profit on a stock that has substantially increased in value.

So it is in a Crap Game. Once you have achieved your goal of a substantial profit on your investment, limit yourself (stop loss order) on how much of it you can lose back without jeopardizing your big percentage of profit. On the other hand, continue to play if your profit continually increases.

Always quit winner once you have doubled your investment, and never try to "break the bank." Good luck.

## A PERSONAL WORD FROM MELVIN POWERS, PUBLISHER, WILSHIRE BOOK COMPANY

My goal is to publish interesting, informative, and inspirational books. You can help me to accomplish this by sending me your answers to the following questions:

Did you enjoy reading this book? Why?

What ideas in the book impressed you most? Have you applied them to your daily life? How?

Is there a chapter that could serve as a theme for an entire book? Explain.

Would you like to read similar books? What additional information would you like them to contain?

If you have an idea for a book, I would welcome discussing it with you. If you have a manuscript in progress, write or call me concerning possible publication.

Melvin Powers
12015 Sherman Road
North Hollywood, California 91605

(818) 765-8579

# MELVIN POWERS SELF-IMPROVEMENT LIBRARY

## ASTROLOGY

____ASTROLOGY—HOW TO CHART YOUR HOROSCOPE  Max Heindel . . . . . . . . . . . . . 7.00
____ASTROLOGY AND SEXUAL ANALYSIS  Morris C. Goodman . . . . . . . . . . . . . . . . . 10.00
____ASTROLOGY AND YOU  Carroll Righter . . . . . . . . . . . . . . . . . . . . . . . . . . . . . . . . 5.00
____ASTROLOGY MADE EASY  Astarte . . . . . . . . . . . . . . . . . . . . . . . . . . . . . . . . . . . . 7.00
____ASTROLOGY, ROMANCE, YOU AND THE STARS  Anthony Norvell . . . . . . . . . . . 10.00
____MY WORLD OF ASTROLOGY  Sydney Omarr . . . . . . . . . . . . . . . . . . . . . . . . . . . . 10.00
____THOUGHT DIAL  Sydney Omarr . . . . . . . . . . . . . . . . . . . . . . . . . . . . . . . . . . . . . 7.00
____WHAT THE STARS REVEAL ABOUT THE MEN IN YOUR LIFE  Thelma White . . . . . . 3.00

## BRIDGE

____BRIDGE BIDDING MADE EASY  Edwin B. Kantar . . . . . . . . . . . . . . . . . . . . . . . . . 15.00
____BRIDGE CONVENTIONS  Edwin B. Kantar . . . . . . . . . . . . . . . . . . . . . . . . . . . . . 10.00
____COMPETITIVE BIDDING IN MODERN BRIDGE  Edgar Kaplan . . . . . . . . . . . . . . 7.00
____DEFENSIVE BRIDGE PLAY COMPLETE  Edwin B Kantar . . . . . . . . . . . . . . . . . . 20.00
____GAMESMAN BRIDGE—PLAY BETTER WITH KANTAR  Edwin B. Kantar . . . . . . . 7.00
____HOW TO IMPROVE YOUR BRIDGE  Alfred Sheinwold . . . . . . . . . . . . . . . . . . . . 7.00
____IMPROVING YOUR BIDDING SKILLS  Edwin B. Kantar . . . . . . . . . . . . . . . . . . . 10.00
____INTRODUCTION TO DECLARER'S PLAY  Edwin B. Kantar . . . . . . . . . . . . . . . . . 7.00
____INTRODUCTION TO DEFENDER'S PLAY  Edwin B. Kantar . . . . . . . . . . . . . . . . . 10.00
____KANTAR FOR THE DEFENSE  Edwin B. Kantar . . . . . . . . . . . . . . . . . . . . . . . . . 10.00
____KANTAR FOR THE DEFENSE VOLUME 2  Edwin B. Kantar . . . . . . . . . . . . . . . . . 10.00
____TEST YOUR BRIDGE PLAY  Edwin B. Kantar . . . . . . . . . . . . . . . . . . . . . . . . . . . 10.00
____VOLUME 2—TEST YOUR BRIDGE PLAY  Edwin B. Kantar . . . . . . . . . . . . . . . . . 10.00
____WINNING DECLARER PLAY  Dorothy Hayden Truscott . . . . . . . . . . . . . . . . . . . 10.00

## BUSINESS, STUDY & REFERENCE

____BRAINSTORMING  Charles Clark . . . . . . . . . . . . . . . . . . . . . . . . . . . . . . . . . . . . 10.00
____CONVERSATION MADE EASY  Elliot Russell . . . . . . . . . . . . . . . . . . . . . . . . . . . . 5.00
____EXAM SECRET  Dennis B. Jackson . . . . . . . . . . . . . . . . . . . . . . . . . . . . . . . . . . 7.00
____FIX-IT BOOK  Arthur Symons . . . . . . . . . . . . . . . . . . . . . . . . . . . . . . . . . . . . . . 2.00
____HOW TO DEVELOP A BETTER SPEAKING VOICE  M. Hellier . . . . . . . . . . . . . . . 5.00
____HOW TO SAVE 50% ON GAS & CAR EXPENSES  Ken Stansbie . . . . . . . . . . . . . 5.00
____HOW TO SELF-PUBLISH YOUR BOOK & MAKE IT A BEST SELLER  Melvin Powers . . 20.00
____INCREASE YOUR LEARNING POWER  Geoffrey A. Dudley . . . . . . . . . . . . . . . . . 5.00
____PRACTICAL GUIDE TO BETTER CONCENTRATION  Melvin Powers . . . . . . . . . . . 5.00
____PUBLIC SPEAKING MADE EASY  Thomas Montalbo . . . . . . . . . . . . . . . . . . . . . 10.00
____7 DAYS TO FASTER READING  William S. Schaill . . . . . . . . . . . . . . . . . . . . . . . 7.00
____SONGWRITER'S RHYMING DICTIONARY  Jane Shaw Whitfield . . . . . . . . . . . . . 10.00
____SPELLING MADE EASY  Lester D. Basch & Dr. Milton Finkelstein . . . . . . . . . . . 3.00
____STUDENT'S GUIDE TO BETTER GRADES  J.A. Rickard . . . . . . . . . . . . . . . . . . . 3.00
____TEST YOURSELF—FIND YOUR HIDDEN TALENT  Jack Shafer . . . . . . . . . . . . . . 3.00
____YOUR WILL & WHAT TO DO ABOUT IT  Attorney Samuel G. King . . . . . . . . . . . . 7.00

## CALLIGRAPHY

____ADVANCED CALLIGRAPHY  Katherine Jeffares . . . . . . . . . . . . . . . . . . . . . . . . . 7.00
____CALLIGRAPHY—THE ART OF BEAUTIFUL WRITING  Katherine Jeffares . . . . . . . . 7.00
____CALLIGRAPHY FOR FUN & PROFIT  Anne Leptich & Jacque Evans . . . . . . . . . . 10.00
____CALLIGRAPHY MADE EASY  Tina Serafini . . . . . . . . . . . . . . . . . . . . . . . . . . . . . 7.00

## CHESS & CHECKERS

____BEGINNER'S GUIDE TO WINNING CHESS  Fred Reinfeld . . . . . . . . . . . . . . . . . . 10.00
____CHESS IN TEN EASY LESSONS  Larry Evans . . . . . . . . . . . . . . . . . . . . . . . . . . . 10.00
____CHESS MADE EASY  Milton L. Hanauer . . . . . . . . . . . . . . . . . . . . . . . . . . . . . . . 5.00
____CHESS PROBLEMS FOR BEGINNERS  Edited by Fred Reinfeld . . . . . . . . . . . . . . 7.00
____CHESS TACTICS FOR BEGINNERS  Edited by Fred Reinfeld . . . . . . . . . . . . . . . . 7.00

____ HOW TO WIN AT CHECKERS  Fred Reinfeld ............................... 7.00
____ 1001 BRILLIANT WAYS TO CHECKMATE  Fred Reinfeld .................... 10.00
____ 1001 WINNING CHESS SACRIFICES & COMBINATIONS  Fred Reinfeld .......... 10.00

## COOKERY & HERBS

____ CULPEPER'S HERBAL REMEDIES  Dr. Nicholas Culpeper .................... 5.00
____ FAST GOURMET COOKBOOK  Poppy Cannon ................................ 2.50
____ HEALING POWER OF HERBS  May Bethel ................................. 5.00
____ HEALING POWER OF NATURAL FOODS  May Bethel ........................ 7.00
____ HERBS FOR HEALTH—HOW TO GROW & USE THEM  Louise Evans Doole ........ 7.00
____ HOME GARDEN COOKBOOK—DELICIOUS NATURAL FOOD RECIPES  Ken Kraft .... 3.00
____ MEATLESS MEAL GUIDE  Tomi Ryan & James H. Ryan, M.D. ................ 4.00
____ VEGETABLE GARDENING FOR BEGINNERS  Hugh Wilberg .................... 2.00
____ VEGETABLES FOR TODAY'S GARDENS  R. Milton Carleton ................. 2.00
____ VEGETARIAN COOKERY  Janet Walker .................................. 10.00
____ VEGETARIAN COOKING MADE EASY & DELECTABLE  Veronica Vezza .......... 3.00

## GAMBLING & POKER

____ HOW TO WIN AT POKER  Terence Reese & Anthony T. Watkins ............ 10.00
____ SCARNE ON DICE  John Scarne ...................................... 15.00
____ WINNING AT CRAPS  Dr. Lloyd T. Commins ............................ 10.00
____ WINNING AT GIN  Chester Wander & Cy Rice ......................... 10.00
____ WINNING AT POKER—AN EXPERT'S GUIDE  John Archer ................... 10.00
____ WINNING AT 21—AN EXPERT'S GUIDE  John Archer ..................... 10.00
____ WINNING POKER SYSTEMS  Norman Zadeh .............................. 10.00

## HEALTH

____ BEE POLLEN  Lynda Lyngheim & Jack Scagnetti ....................... 5.00
____ COPING WITH ALZHEIMER'S  Rose Oliver, Ph.D. & Francis Bock, Ph.D. .... 10.00
____ DR. LINDNER'S POINT SYSTEM FOOD PROGRAM  Peter G Lindner, M.D. ..... 2.00
____ HELP YOURSELF TO BETTER SIGHT  Margaret Darst Corbett ............. 7.00
____ HOW YOU CAN STOP SMOKING PERMANENTLY  Ernest Caldwell ............. 5.00
____ MIND OVER PLATTER  Peter G Lindner, M.D. .......................... 5.00
____ NATURE'S WAY TO NUTRITION & VIBRANT HEALTH  Robert J. Scrutton .... 3.00
____ NEW CARBOHYDRATE DIET COUNTER  Patti Lopez-Pereira ................ 2.00
____ REFLEXOLOGY  Dr. Maybelle Segal .................................. 7.00
____ REFLEXOLOGY FOR GOOD HEALTH  Anna Kaye & Don C. Matchan ........... 10.00
____ 30 DAYS TO BEAUTIFUL LEGS  Dr. Marc Selner ....................... 3.00
____ WONDER WITHIN  Thomas S. Coyle, M.D. ............................. 10.00
____ YOU CAN LEARN TO RELAX  Dr. Samuel Gutwirth ...................... 5.00

## HOBBIES

____ BEACHCOMBING FOR BEGINNERS  Norman Hickin ........................ 2.00
____ BLACKSTONE'S MODERN CARD TRICKS  Harry Blackstone ................ 7.00
____ BLACKSTONE'S SECRETS OF MAGIC  Harry Blackstone .................. 7.00
____ COIN COLLECTING FOR BEGINNERS  Burton Hobson & Fred Reinfeld ...... 7.00
____ ENTERTAINING WITH ESP  Tony 'Doc' Shiels ......................... 2.00
____ 400 FASCINATING MAGIC TRICKS YOU CAN DO  Howard Thurston ......... 7.00
____ HOW I TURN JUNK INTO FUN AND PROFIT  Sari ........................ 3.00
____ HOW TO WRITE A HIT SONG AND SELL IT  Tommy Boyce ................ 10.00
____ MAGIC FOR ALL AGES  Walter Gibson ................................ 7.00
____ PLANTING A TREE  TreePeople with Andy & Katie Lipkis ............. 13.00
____ STAMP COLLECTING FOR BEGINNERS  Burton Hobson .................... 3.00

## HORSE PLAYERS' WINNING GUIDES

____ BETTING HORSES TO WIN  Les Conklin ............................... 10.00
____ ELIMINATE THE LOSERS  Bob McKnight ............................... 5.00
____ HOW TO PICK WINNING HORSES  Bob McKnight ......................... 5.00
____ HOW TO WIN AT THE RACES  Sam (The Genius) Lewin .................. 5.00

\_\_\_ HOW YOU CAN BEAT THE RACES  Jack Kavanagh . . . . . . . . . . . . . . . . . . . . . . . . . . . 5.00
\_\_\_ MAKING MONEY AT THE RACES  David Barr . . . . . . . . . . . . . . . . . . . . . . . . . . . . . 7.00
\_\_\_ PAYDAY AT THE RACES  Les Conklin . . . . . . . . . . . . . . . . . . . . . . . . . . . . . . . . . 7.00
\_\_\_ SMART HANDICAPPING MADE EASY  William Bauman . . . . . . . . . . . . . . . . . . . . . 5.00
\_\_\_ SUCCESS AT THE HARNESS RACES  Barry Meadow . . . . . . . . . . . . . . . . . . . . . . . 7.00

### HUMOR

\_\_\_ HOW TO FLATTEN YOUR TUSH  Coach Marge Reardon . . . . . . . . . . . . . . . . . . . . . 2.00
\_\_\_ JOKE TELLER'S HANDBOOK  Bob Orben . . . . . . . . . . . . . . . . . . . . . . . . . . . . . . . 7.00
\_\_\_ JOKES FOR ALL OCCASIONS  Al Schock . . . . . . . . . . . . . . . . . . . . . . . . . . . . . . . 7.00
\_\_\_ 2,000 NEW LAUGHS FOR SPEAKERS  Bob Orben . . . . . . . . . . . . . . . . . . . . . . . . . 7.00
\_\_\_ 2,400 JOKES TO BRIGHTEN YOUR SPEECHES  Robert Orben . . . . . . . . . . . . . . . 10.00
\_\_\_ 2,500 JOKES TO START'EM LAUGHING  Bob Orben . . . . . . . . . . . . . . . . . . . . . . . 10.00

### HYPNOTISM

\_\_\_ CHILDBIRTH WITH HYPNOSIS  William S. Kroger, M.D. . . . . . . . . . . . . . . . . . . . . . . 5.00
\_\_\_ HOW YOU CAN BOWL BETTER USING SELF-HYPNOSIS  Jack Heise . . . . . . . . . . 7.00
\_\_\_ HOW YOU CAN PLAY BETTER GOLF USING SELF-HYPNOSIS  Jack Heise . . . . . . . . 3.00
\_\_\_ HYPNOSIS AND SELF-HYPNOSIS  Bernard Hollander, M.D. . . . . . . . . . . . . . . . . . . . 7.00
\_\_\_ HYPNOTISM (Originally published 1893)  Carl Sextus . . . . . . . . . . . . . . . . . . . . . . . 5.00
\_\_\_ HYPNOTISM MADE EASY  Dr. Ralph Winn . . . . . . . . . . . . . . . . . . . . . . . . . . . . . . 10.00
\_\_\_ HYPNOTISM MADE PRACTICAL  Louis Orton . . . . . . . . . . . . . . . . . . . . . . . . . . . . . 5.00
\_\_\_ MODERN HYPNOSIS  Lesley Kuhn & Salvatore Russo, Ph.D. . . . . . . . . . . . . . . . . . . 5.00
\_\_\_ NEW CONCEPTS OF HYPNOSIS  Bernard C. Gindes, M.D. . . . . . . . . . . . . . . . . . . 10.00
\_\_\_ NEW SELF-HYPNOSIS  Paul Adams . . . . . . . . . . . . . . . . . . . . . . . . . . . . . . . . . . 10.00
\_\_\_ POST-HYPNOTIC INSTRUCTIONS—SUGGESTIONS FOR THERAPY  Arnold Furst . . . 10.00
\_\_\_ PRACTICAL GUIDE TO SELF-HYPNOSIS  Melvin Powers . . . . . . . . . . . . . . . . . . . . 10.00
\_\_\_ PRACTICAL HYPNOTISM  Philip Magonet, M.D. . . . . . . . . . . . . . . . . . . . . . . . . . . . 3.00
\_\_\_ SECRETS OF HYPNOTISM  S.J. Van Pelt, M.D. . . . . . . . . . . . . . . . . . . . . . . . . . . . 5.00
\_\_\_ SELF-HYPNOSIS—A CONDITIONED-RESPONSE TECHNIQUE  Laurence Sparks . . . . 7.00
\_\_\_ SELF-HYPNOSIS—ITS THEORY, TECHNIQUE & APPLICATION  Melvin Powers . . . . . 7.00
\_\_\_ THERAPY THROUGH HYPNOSIS  Edited by Raphael H. Rhodes . . . . . . . . . . . . . . . 5.00

### JUDAICA

\_\_\_ SERVICE OF THE HEART  Evelyn Garfiel, Ph.D. . . . . . . . . . . . . . . . . . . . . . . . . . . 10.00
\_\_\_ STORY OF ISRAEL IN COINS  Jean & Maurice Gould . . . . . . . . . . . . . . . . . . . . . . . 2.00
\_\_\_ STORY OF ISRAEL IN STAMPS  Maxim & Gabriel Shamir . . . . . . . . . . . . . . . . . . . . 1.00
\_\_\_ TONGUE OF THE PROPHETS  Robert St. John . . . . . . . . . . . . . . . . . . . . . . . . . . 10.00

### JUST FOR WOMEN

\_\_\_ COSMOPOLITAN'S GUIDE TO MARVELOUS MEN  Foreword by Helen Gurley Brown . . 3.00
\_\_\_ COSMOPOLITAN'S HANG-UP HANDBOOK  Foreword by Helen Gurley Brown . . . . . . . . 4.00
\_\_\_ COSMOPOLITAN'S LOVE BOOK—A GUIDE TO ECSTASY IN BED . . . . . . . . . . . . . . 7.00
\_\_\_ COSMOPOLITAN'S NEW ETIQUETTE GUIDE  Foreword by Helen Gurley Brown . . . . . . 4.00
\_\_\_ I AM A COMPLEAT WOMAN  Doris Hagopian & Karen O'Connor Sweeney . . . . . . . . . 3.00
\_\_\_ JUST FOR WOMEN—A GUIDE TO THE FEMALE BODY  Richard E. Sand M.D. . . . . . . 5.00
\_\_\_ NEW APPROACHES TO SEX IN MARRIAGE  John E. Eichenlaub, M.D. . . . . . . . . . . . 3.00
\_\_\_ SEXUALLY ADEQUATE FEMALE  Frank S. Caprio, M.D. . . . . . . . . . . . . . . . . . . . . . 3.00
\_\_\_ SEXUALLY FULFILLED WOMAN  Dr. Rachel Copelan . . . . . . . . . . . . . . . . . . . . . . . 5.00

### MARRIAGE, SEX & PARENTHOOD

\_\_\_ ABILITY TO LOVE  Dr. Allan Fromme . . . . . . . . . . . . . . . . . . . . . . . . . . . . . . . . . . 7.00
\_\_\_ GUIDE TO SUCCESSFUL MARRIAGE  Drs. Albert Ellis & Robert Harper . . . . . . . . . . 10.00
\_\_\_ HOW TO RAISE AN EMOTIONALLY HEALTHY, HAPPY CHILD  Albert Ellis, Ph.D. . . . . 10.00
\_\_\_ PARENT SURVIVAL TRAINING  Marvin Silverman, Ed.D. & David Lustig, Ph.D. . . . . . . 10.00
\_\_\_ POTENCY MIRACLE  Uri P. Peles, M.D. . . . . . . . . . . . . . . . . . . . . . . . . . . . . . . . . 10.00
\_\_\_ SEX WITHOUT GUILT  Albert Ellis, Ph.D. . . . . . . . . . . . . . . . . . . . . . . . . . . . . . . . 7.00
\_\_\_ SEXUALLY ADEQUATE MALE  Frank S. Caprio, M.D. . . . . . . . . . . . . . . . . . . . . . . . 3.00
\_\_\_ SEXUALLY FULFILLED MAN  Dr. Rachel Copelan . . . . . . . . . . . . . . . . . . . . . . . . . . 5.00

\_\_\_ KNIGHT IN RUSTY ARMOR (Hard Cover) Robert Fisher . . . . . . . . . . . . . . . . . . . 10.00
\_\_\_ LEFT-HANDED PEOPLE Michael Barsley . . . . . . . . . . . . . . . . . . . . . . . . . . . . 5.00
\_\_\_ MAGIC IN YOUR MIND U.S. Andersen . . . . . . . . . . . . . . . . . . . . . . . . . . . . 10.00
\_\_\_ MAGIC OF THINKING SUCCESS Dr. David J. Schwartz . . . . . . . . . . . . . . . . . . 10.00
\_\_\_ MAGIC POWER OF YOUR MIND Walter M. Germain . . . . . . . . . . . . . . . . . . . . 10.00
\_\_\_ NEVER UNDERESTIMATE THE SELLING POWER OF A WOMAN Dottie Walters . . . . . 7.00
\_\_\_ PRINCESS WHO BELIEVED IN FAIRY TALES Marcia Grad . . . . . . . . . . . . . . . . . 10.00
\_\_\_ PSYCHO-CYBERNETICS Maxwell Maltz, M.D. . . . . . . . . . . . . . . . . . . . . . . . . 10.00
\_\_\_ PSYCHOLOGY OF HANDWRITING Nadya Olyanova . . . . . . . . . . . . . . . . . . . . 10.00
\_\_\_ SALES CYBERNETICS Brian Adams . . . . . . . . . . . . . . . . . . . . . . . . . . . . . 10.00
\_\_\_ SECRET OF SECRETS U.S. Andersen . . . . . . . . . . . . . . . . . . . . . . . . . . . . 10.00
\_\_\_ SECRET POWER OF THE PYRAMIDS U.S. Andersen . . . . . . . . . . . . . . . . . . . . 7.00
\_\_\_ SELF-THERAPY FOR THE STUTTERER Malcolm Frazer . . . . . . . . . . . . . . . . . . 3.00
\_\_\_ STOP COMMITTING VOICE SUICIDE Morton Cooper, Ph.D. . . . . . . . . . . . . . . . 10.00
\_\_\_ SUCCESS CYBERNETICS U.S. Andersen . . . . . . . . . . . . . . . . . . . . . . . . . . 7.00
\_\_\_ 10 DAYS TO A GREAT NEW LIFE William E. Edwards . . . . . . . . . . . . . . . . . . . 3.00
\_\_\_ THINK AND GROW RICH Napoleon Hill . . . . . . . . . . . . . . . . . . . . . . . . . . . 10.00
\_\_\_ THINK LIKE A WINNER Walter Doyle Staples, Ph.D. . . . . . . . . . . . . . . . . . . . . 15.00
\_\_\_ THREE MAGIC WORDS U.S. Andersen . . . . . . . . . . . . . . . . . . . . . . . . . . . 12.00
\_\_\_ TREASURY OF COMFORT Edited by Rabbi Sidney Greenberg . . . . . . . . . . . . . . 10.00
\_\_\_ TREASURY OF THE ART OF LIVING Edited by Rabbi Sidney Greenberg . . . . . . . . . 10.00
\_\_\_ WHAT YOUR HANDWRITING REVEALS Albert E. Hughes . . . . . . . . . . . . . . . . . 4.00
\_\_\_ WINNING WITH YOUR VOICE Morton Cooper, Ph.D. . . . . . . . . . . . . . . . . . . . 10.00
\_\_\_ WONDER WITHIN Thomas F. Coyle, M.D. . . . . . . . . . . . . . . . . . . . . . . . . . 10.00
\_\_\_ YOUR SUBCONSCIOUS POWER Charles M. Simmons . . . . . . . . . . . . . . . . . . 7.00

### SPORTS

\_\_\_ BILLIARDS—POCKET • CAROM • THREE CUSHION Clive Cottingham, Jr. . . . . . . . . 10.00
\_\_\_ COMPLETE GUIDE TO FISHING Vlad Evanoff . . . . . . . . . . . . . . . . . . . . . . . . 2.00
\_\_\_ HOW TO IMPROVE YOUR RACQUETBALL Lubarsky, Kaufman & Scagnetti . . . . . . . . 5.00
\_\_\_ HOW TO WIN AT POCKET BILLIARDS Edward D. Knuchell . . . . . . . . . . . . . . . . 10.00
\_\_\_ JOY OF WALKING Jack Scagnetti . . . . . . . . . . . . . . . . . . . . . . . . . . . . . . 3.00
\_\_\_ RACQUETBALL FOR WOMEN Toni Hudson, Jack Scagnetti & Vince Rondone . . . . . . 3.00
\_\_\_ SECRET OF BOWLING STRIKES Dawson Taylor . . . . . . . . . . . . . . . . . . . . . . 5.00
\_\_\_ SOCCER—THE GAME & HOW TO PLAY IT Gary Rosenthal . . . . . . . . . . . . . . . . 7.00
\_\_\_ STARTING SOCCER Edward F Dolan, Jr. . . . . . . . . . . . . . . . . . . . . . . . . . . 5.00

### TENNIS LOVERS' LIBRARY

\_\_\_ HOW TO BEAT BETTER TENNIS PLAYERS Loring Fiske . . . . . . . . . . . . . . . . . . 4.00
\_\_\_ PSYCH YOURSELF TO BETTER TENNIS Dr. Walter A. Luszki . . . . . . . . . . . . . . . 2.00
\_\_\_ TENNIS FOR BEGINNERS Dr. H.A. Murray . . . . . . . . . . . . . . . . . . . . . . . . . 2.00
\_\_\_ WEEKEND TENNIS—HOW TO HAVE FUN & WIN AT THE SAME TIME Bill Talbert . . . 3.00

### WILSHIRE PET LIBRARY

\_\_\_ DOG TRAINING MADE EASY & FUN John W. Kellogg . . . . . . . . . . . . . . . . . . . 5.00
\_\_\_ HOW TO BRING UP YOUR PET DOG Kurt Unkelbach . . . . . . . . . . . . . . . . . . . 2.00
\_\_\_ HOW TO RAISE & TRAIN YOUR PUPPY Jeff Griffen . . . . . . . . . . . . . . . . . . . . 5.00

Available from your bookstore or directly from Melvin Powers.
Please add $2.00 shipping and handling for each book ordered.

## Melvin Powers
12015 Sherman Road, No. Hollywood, California 91605

**For our complete catalog, visit our Web site at http://www.mpowers.com.**